# TREES
## of Australia

H. Oakman

THE JACARANDA PRESS

D1745154

First published 1970 by
JACARANDA PRESS PTY LTD
46 Douglas Street, Milton, Q.
142 Victoria Road, Marrickville, N.S.W.
162 Albert Road, South Melbourne, Vic.

Filmtypeset by Press Etching Pty Ltd, Brisbane
Printed in Hong Kong

© H. Oakman 1970

National Library of Australia
Card Number and ISBN 7016 0350 X

# CONTENTS

# INTRODUCTION

Some of our most cherished memories are often associated with trees; perhaps we recall the flowering Gum in the schoolground that suddenly burst into colour, the Moreton Bay Fig trees that provided shade in the sportsfield, or the Silky Oaks and She Oaks that lined the watercourse where we picnicked. Everyone must surely have been emotionally stirred at seeing our giant Eucalypts for the first time and enchanted with the lush beauty of a rain forest. I venture to say that all of these memories are pleasant ones and that, probably subconsciously, we all love trees.

In this booklet only a few of the several hundred species of Australian trees have been described. As far as possible, a representative selection has been made from the various plant families, the useful or ornamental and the rare trees that grow in the different regions of this continent.

Most of Australia's trees grow on the southern and eastern fringes of the continent They originate from three broad sources: the Antarctic, Australia and South-east Asia.

For the purposes of classification, plants are generally grouped into botanical families but they can also be grouped according to their geographic distribution, their countries of origin and in numerous other ways. Trees can similarly be classified into such arbitrary groups as for example, fruit trees, rain-forest trees, flowering trees, shade trees, etc. In this booklet they are arranged alphabetically.

Plant communities in nature are not stable; they change constantly, often almost unnoticeably until, over a period of many years, an ultimate or climax vegetation is established. This will vary according to local conditions. An original grass cover, for example, may enable shrubs to germinate and become predominant. The shrubs can in turn provide suitable conditions for trees to establish themselves. Where soil and rainfall are suitable, the process will produce a forest vegetation that remains fairly stable.

The plants of a climax vegetation, generally tend to group themselves into communities under the influence of such variable factors as rock formation, soil, bog conditions, slopes, exposure and local fauna. An approximate reproduction of these conditions is most likely to produce the best results for those interested in tree culture.

The Australian vegetation is comprised of five fairly distinct groups. *Desert* vegetation is typified by Salt Bush and some Acacias living under arid conditions where a spasmodic five inch rainfall may sometimes be followed by dry spells of up to two years. In *Grassland* grass predominates, with occasional shrubs or herbs. In *Scrub* the Heaths, Mallee, Brigalow, Tea-tree, Banksia and Casuarina predominate. *Open Forest* occurs in areas with at least a twenty-inch rainfall. Most of the gums are found in this group. The *Rain Forests* consist of dense, jungle-like growth made up of tall close-growing trees, ferns, climbers and epiphytic plants (Orchids and Staghorns). Associated with both types of forest are areas of coniferous forests.

*Eucalypt Forests* are the dominant type in the leathery-leaved (sclerophyll) forests which constitute about 95 per cent of the commercial forests of Australia. They grow on all kinds of soils but only in regions where the rainfall is above twenty inches a year. They produce some of the world's best hardwoods which are noted for their strength, durability, toughness and hardness.

Their principal use is in building construction. They vary from 320 feet in height, e.g. Mountain Ash (*Eucalyptus regnans*) and the West Australian Karri (*E. diversicolor*)—forest giants that have been known to log 200 tons of timber from one tree—to Mallees that grow to an average height of only twenty feet and which can withstand hot and parched desert conditions where there is an average rainfall of less than ten inches.

The Mallees have little commercial value; they are used mostly for fuel or for extraction of their essential oils. They are characterised by a clump of slender stems, dwarf growth and their tremendous ability to survive under adverse conditions; fire and drought result in only a temporary setback. Many of the shrubby Mallees are very decorative when in full bloom and are becoming increasingly popular in ornamental horticulture. As a rule they grow in areas of winter rain.

A few Eucalypts can withstand extremes of exposure or cold such as we find in the Australian Alps where the Snow Gum (*E. niphophila*) flourishes. Others are beautiful flowering trees (*E. ficifolia*), honey producers (*E. melliodora*) or contain essential oils (*E. citriodora*).

The Eucalypts are roughly classified into Bloodwoods, Blue Gums, Red Gums, Stringybarks, Ash, Peppermints,

3

Boxes, Ironbarks and Mallees. This classification is according to the bark or timber. The genus was named in 1788 by Charles-Louis L'Héritier de Brutelle. Their botanic classification is quite difficult and depends on various floral and structural features that are not sufficiently constant for indisputable determination and as a result there has been some confusion in names. Positive identification is often difficult because they hybridize readily and can vary considerably in different localities. Some authorities claim that there are approximately 600 species of Eucalypts, of which some 60 are Mallees; others limit the number to 400 species.

All of the Eucalypts have foliage that reduces water evaporation by the volatilization of essential oils. The leaves have a thick cuticle and usually hang vertically. The stalks turn so that only the leaf edge faces towards the sun. Young leaves (i.e. juvenile leaves) are almost invariably quite distinct from mature leaves in shape, size and colour.

Associated with the hardwood forests are Turpentines (*Syncarpia* spp.) and Apple (*Angophora* spp.) which closely resemble the Eucalypts; the Wattles (*Acacia*), and the She Oaks (*Casuarina*), both of which produce commercial timbers but only in small sizes. Some Wattles produce tannin which has been the commercial source of tan bark (*Acacia pycnantha*) while others, such as the Mulga (*Acacia aneura*), are good fodder trees.

The better known areas of *Rain Forest* include some parts of Western Tasmania, areas from south of Lake King, Victoria, through to the Illawarra Range, Braidwood, in some of the deep Blue Mountain gorges, and

Barrington Tops, Dorrigo, Richmond River, Murwill-umbah, and northward to Cape York. All of these forests are coastal and their maximum distance inland is less than 100 miles. Their annual rainfall can vary from 50 to 120 inches.

The Australian rain forests are sometimes aptly referred to as jungle or brush. They can be extremely difficult to penetrate without cutting a track through the dense or tangled undergrowth. They contain a great variety of trees—some 200 genera in fact—mostly growing as mixed specimens rather than in groups of any one variety.

The rain forests often occupy sheltered valleys associated with watercourses and as a rule change abruptly from their adjoining open (*Eucalyptus*) forests. Growth is always luxurious, particularly in the warmer and moister regions where ancient and young trees as well as tall Palms grow within a few feet of each other. Many tree and palm trunks support vines or epiphytes such as Elkhorns, Staghorns, Orchids, Crows Nest and various ferns. The latter, including tree-ferns, can also form a large part of the forest ground cover.

The rainfall in these forest areas is chiefly between December and March (summer) and is of a tropical nature. The soils vary considerably but are usually enriched by continuous coverings of leaf mould.

The *Eucalyptus* forests are fairly fire-resistant and recover rapidly, but rain forests succumb to fire. These fires are generally man-induced as the forests are too moist to ignite spontaneously except in severe droughts.

The average height of a rain forest is 120 feet. Most of

the trees are evergreen but some notable exceptions are White Cedar (*Melia azedarach*) and Red Cedar (*Toona cedrela*). Leaves, as a rule, are large, compound or lobed, and held horizontally. Many of the younger leaves are tinted and the juvenile foliage occasionally takes on a deep pink coloration (e.g. Lillypilly, *Eugenia* spp., and Maiden's Blush, *Euroschinus falcatus*).

Many rain forest trees have fluted trunks, or buttresses, which are upright extensions of the lower trunk and roots, forming an effective support for the trees.

Most of the softwoods of the Australian timber trade are obtained from the rain forest trees. Many of these are renowned for their colour, grain or pleasant odour.

Compared with the hardwoods and the rain forest trees, the *Australian Conifers* are represented by only a few genera, but the areas covered by them are quite extensive. Larger trees such as Kauri and Hoop Pine are confined to coastal regions of good soil and a rainfall of about fifty inches. Inland there are large tracts of dry forest country with rainfalls below twenty inches that are covered with 'Pines' of the *Callitris* group (Cypress Pine).

Growth under Australian conditions is more erratic than in temperate climates where the alternation between summer and winter induces annual growth rings that enable the age of a tree to be accurately assessed. Intermittent droughts prevent the growth rings from indicating a regular time cycle. It has been established, however, that some Kauri Pines which have grown to an eight-foot diameter under ideal conditions were 400 years old.

The better known groups of Australian conifers are *Callitris* (Cypress Pines), *Araucarias* (Hoop Pine, Bunya Pine); *Agathis* (Kauri) and *Podocarpus* (She Pine). The natural stands of these trees have nearly all disappeared because of the great demand for their commercially valuable softwoods.

The Forestry Departments of each state are replanting large areas with softwoods and hardwoods. Throughout the world there is an awareness of the need for replanting forests, and in the U.S.A. alone, over 200 million trees are planted every year; among these are many species that are indigenous to Australia.

Australia has occasionally been described as a land of tree-haters. That is too harsh a generalization. But it is true that very few Australians fully appreciate the magnificence of their tree heritage. In some places, only a few decades separate us from the early colonizers who cleared the land for quick profits and a speedy return to their homeland. In others the time gap is greater, but we have failed to make amends. The ruthless tree destruction of our pioneer forefathers has left many thousands of acres of this continent so completely treeless that even the uncaring are beginning to realize that we should conserve our remaining trees and replant as many as possible.

The value of trees to a farmer is so obvious that one wonders what prompted the lust for their destruction. Strip the land of trees and the absorbent leaf covering that it had under forest conditions becomes parched soil that gullies rapidly during rain or blows away in the wind. If only a chain-wide strip of trees was retained as a separation between paddocks, they would provide timber for structural purposes, fuel, wind-breaks, shade for animals, a refuge for birds, honey for the bees and—for good measure—improve the landscape.

Destruction is always so very much easier than restoration. Australia is not a land of forests—in fact only 2 per cent of this continent is forest, as against over-populated Japan's 59 per cent, U.S.S.R. 59 per cent, Canada 32 per cent, Great Britain 6 per cent, and Finland, 73 per cent.

It is time to take stock of our trees. They are necessary to our existence, both economically and aesthetically. The more we can learn to appreciate them, the more we will benefit from them.

# ACKNOWLEDGMENTS

I wish to thank Mr R. K. Mair, Director and Chief Botanist of the Sydney Royal Botanic Gardens, for checking the botanical and common names of the 60 trees described in the text; also Dr J. S. Beard, Director of Kings Park and Botanic Gardens, Perth, for the colour transparency of the Western Australian Christmas Tree, and John Coker for the transparency of Mountain Ebony.

# ALPINE SNOW GUM

*Eucalyptus niphophila* (Family Myrtaceae)

HABITAT: The sub-alpine areas of Victoria and N.S.W.
as far north as Queensland; the Victorian Alps and
Mt Kosciusko at elevations between 3500 and 6500
feet.

SIZE: Average height is 20 feet, usually with several
twisted stems.

DESCRIPTION: The bark is smooth, powdery white often
with cream, grey or pale pink markings in irregular
patches; extends to the branch tips; the branchlets
are smooth, reddish brown. Mature leaves are alternate, 5 inches long by $\frac{3}{4}$ inch wide, lanceolate, with
$\frac{3}{4}$ inch stalks. They are mid-green, fleshy, glossy on
both sides with almost parallel venation. Flowers are
in clusters of 3 to 7, close to the branchlets; anthers
are creamy white. Fruit is a globose or pear-shaped
capsule, short-stalked, usually covered with a grey
bloom.

TIMBER: As a rule only in small sizes; light brown, not
very hard and has gum veins; used for fence posts.

GENERAL NOTES: This tree almost invariably has a
gnarled appearance, no doubt due to the weight of
snow on the branches during the winter months.
Grows in exposed positions on rocky slopes but is
very often disinclined to survive for long when planted
as an ornamental. Difficult to distinguish from the
White Sallee or Snow Gum, *Eucalyptus pauciflora*.

# BARKLYA

*Barklya syringifolia*             (Family Leguminosae)

HABITAT: From the Richmond River, N.S.W., to Wide Bay, Queensland, in open forests and in rain forests, generally in deep soils. The genus is limited to one species which is found only in Australia.

SIZE: Can grow as high as 60 feet with a stem diameter of 2 feet but as a rule it is a medium-sized tree occasionally with a multiple stem.

DESCRIPTION: The young shoots and inflorescences are sometimes covered with rusty hairs but as a rule the foliage is smooth, shiny and deep green in colour. Leaves are alternate, heart-shaped or broad at the base; 3 inches long with a 2 inch stalk. The flowers are orange or apricot, in dense terminal racemes 6 inches long forming a large terminal inflorescence superficially resembling a cluster of bottlebrush blooms. Individual flowers are $\frac{1}{4}$ to $\frac{1}{2}$ inch long; these are followed by 2 to 3 inch seed pods containing 1 or 3 flat seeds.

TIMBER: Hard, blackish-grey, close-grained and tough; suitable for tool handles.

GENERAL NOTES: The *Barklya* makes a magnificent colour display for about three weeks in January/February. During that time its foliage is almost obscured beneath a canopy of apricot coloured flowers. For the remainder of the year the attractive green foliage provides dense shade. It needs good conditions for satisfactory growth.

# BLACK BEAN

*Castanospermum australe*          (Family Leguminosae)

HABITAT: The north coast of N.S.W. and coastal Queensland. It is plentiful along watercourses and in the rain forests. This genus is confined to Australia.

SIZE: Grows to 70 feet with a stem diameter up to 3 feet. Columnar but sometimes flanged at the base.

DESCRIPTION: Bark is dark grey, thin, compact and fairly smooth. Leaves are up to 2 feet long, with 10 to 15 leaflets 5 inches long, elliptical. Flowers are on axillary racemes, about 4 inches long and one inch in diameter, somewhat pea-shaped, fleshy, and are borne on last year's wood; colour is yellow, orange and coral-red. Seeds are in woody boat-shaped pods up to 10 inches long which contain 2 to 5 two-inch diameter spherical seeds that were a source of food for the Aborigines. Dr T. L. Bancroft, however, claimed that the seeds were poisonous. There is also reason to believe that they are injurious to stock.

TIMBER: Strongly resembles Walnut. It is beautifully figured and is regarded as one of the finest cabinet hardwoods. It is straight-grained, takes a high polish and is in great demand as a plywood veneer.

GENERAL NOTES: The Black Bean was one of the first native trees to be brought into cultivation as it is suited to all but the driest and coldest regions. It partially defoliates in November just prior to flowering. Sometimes the yellow and red flowers are quite spectacular but under lush growing conditions the foliage is retained and obscures the flowers.

14

# BLACK CYPRESS PINE

*Callitris endlicheri*                    (Family Cupressaceae)

HABITAT: The Southern Alps, upper Murray River, the Dividing Range and into Queensland, generally in shallow, rocky soils.

SIZE: Attains a height of 50 feet and a stem diameter of nearly 2 feet.

DESCRIPTION: Stem is central and tapering; branching is dense from the ground up in the form of a sharply pointed cone. Bark is dark grey to charcoal, rough and scaly, furrowed and ridged. Leaves are in whorls of 3 or 4, reduced to tiny scales. Male flowers (amenta) are solitary, minute and compact, at the tips of the branchlets. Female cones are stalkless, woody, about $\frac{1}{2}$ inch in size with the 3 larger valves curved outwards; they contain winged seeds.

TIMBER: Marketed as Cypress Pine; aromatic, light and durable, white-ant resistant; often has small knots. Used in building as a general timber, for interior fittings, house stumps, piles and for sheathing punts.

GENERAL NOTES: Previously known as *C. calcarata*, Black Pine or Mountain Pine. Develops into a shapely cone with dense, sometimes ridged foliage that retains its bright olive-green colour all the year round. In its native habitat it usually grows in pure stands and flourishes on hard stony ridges that are regularly subjected to severe frosts.

# BLACKWOOD

*Acacia melanoxylon* (Family Leguminosae)

HABITAT: Tasmania, South Australia, Victoria, southern N.S.W. and into the tablelands: generally at altitudes of up to 3500 feet with a rainfall of between 30 and 70 inches.

SIZE: Will reach up to 100 feet with a stem diameter of 2 to 4 feet but is generally half this size.

DESCRIPTION: The bark is dark grey, hard, has vertical fissures and extends to the tips of the branches. The juvenile leaves are bipinnate with 15 to 20 pairs of leaflets; adult leaves (phyllodes) are lanceolate, curved, about 4 inches long, leathery, the main veins longitudinal. Flowers are in spikes of up to 30, pale to deep yellow, globular blooms. The pods are contorted, dark brown and contain up to 10 small oval seeds.

TIMBER: Yellow to pale brown, close-grained, works well and takes a high polish. Used as a veneer and in cabinet work. Regarded as one of the best of the Australian ornamental timbers.

GENERAL NOTES: Develops a rounded crown when grown as a solitary specimen and makes an excellent shade tree for districts that have severe frosts. Unlike most wattles, it is long lived.

# BOTTLE TREE

*Brachychiton rupestre*                    (Family Sterculiaceae)

HABITAT: Limited to Queensland in the Darling Downs
and Burnett districts, also in the drier scrubs south of
Rockhampton.

SIZE: Attains a height of 50 feet. Stem is bottle-shaped,
the lower part up to 6 feet in diameter; the upper part
carries a dense head of foliage.

DESCRIPTION: Bark is green or brown, furrowed, fibrous
and was used by the Aborigines to make fishing nets.
Leaves are alternate, variable in shape with one-inch
stalks. Young leaves are divided into from 3 to 9
segments, larger leaves entire and in clusters or in
3 segments joined close to the base. Flowers are in
panicles in the forks of the leaves; male and female
flowers and occasionally bi-sexual flowers are on the
one tree. Fruit is a pod composed of 3 to 5 follicles
containing up to 15 seeds, $\frac{1}{4}$ inch in size.

TIMBER: Wood is very soft and of no commercial value.

GENERAL NOTES: The Bottle Tree is sometimes used for
fodder, even the branches being edible. Because of this,
as well as its quaint shape, many farmers refrain from
destroying these trees when clearing their land and
groups of bottle trees in cultivation paddocks are a
unique sight. The common name has prompted the
erroneous belief that the trunk contains potable water;
the mucilaginous pith was, however, used by the
Aborigines as a thirst quencher; they also ate the roots
and seeds.

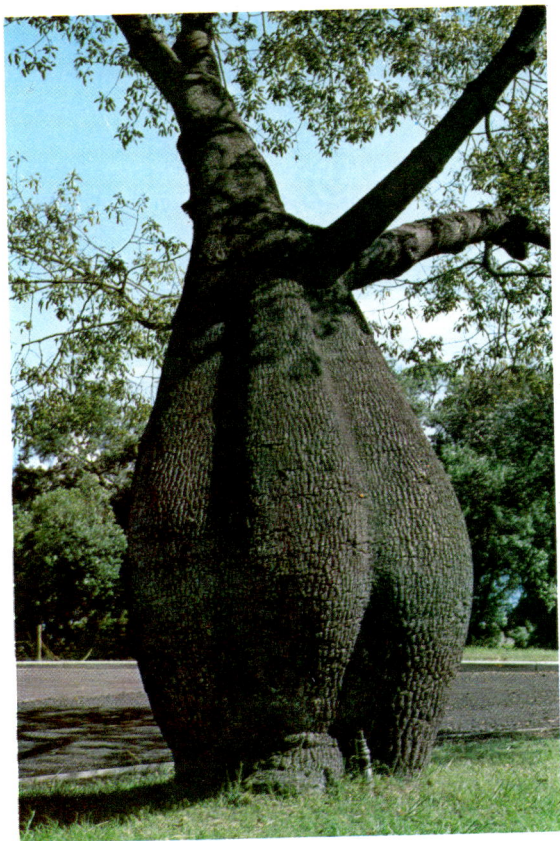

# BROAD-LEAVED PAPERBARK
*Melaleuca quinquenervia* (Family Myrtaceae)

HABITAT: In swamplands and low-lying areas, eastern
Australia, Queensland, Northern Territory and up to
Malaya.

SIZE: Grows to 50 feet with a stem diameter of 2 feet.

DESCRIPTION: Bark is thick, creamy-white in thin, papery
layers which strip off readily; it is often used for lining
hanging baskets. Aboriginal women used it to wrap
their children in, as well as for bedding and for
water-proofing their gunyahs. Leaves are alternate,
lanceolate, rigid, 4 inches long; they contain up to
2 per cent of oil (commercially known as Cajuput)
which is obtained by distillation. Flower spikes superficially resemble small bottlebrushes, yellowish-green
in colour, on terminal spikes with separated flowers
with bunches of stamens $\frac{1}{2}$ inch long. Seed pod is
globular, containing a large number of minute seeds.

TIMBER: Pinkish-grey, close-grained, very hard but has a
tendency to crack; useful for posts in damp places
where it lasts particularly well; often used for ship
timbers and boat knees; white-ant resistant.

GENERAL NOTES: Often develops uneven, multiple stems
which can give it a picturesque appearance particularly when situated in shallow water. It is popularly
believed that if the young leaves are bruised in water,
the resulting fluid relieves headaches and acts as a
tonic.

# BROWN PINE

*Podocarpus elatus*              (Family Podocarpaceae)

HABITAT: The brushes and jungles on the east coast of Australia from Illawarra, N.S.W., to Cairns, north Queensland.

SIZE: Under forest conditions it grows to 100 feet with a stem diameter of 2 feet, but seldom more than 50 feet when grown in the open.

DESCRIPTION: Occasionally the trunk is buttressed or irregularly channelled. Bark is dark-brown, papery in texture and grooved in vertical strips. Leaves are narrow, usually 4 inches long by $\frac{1}{4}$ inch wide, shiny and dark green. Male and female flowers are on different trees; the female flowers are in the axils of the leaves and after fertilization produce a bluish-black plum-like fruit 1 inch in diameter with a seed at the tip of the fruit which is claimed to be edible.

TIMBER: Known as Brown Pine in the timber trade. Colour is golden-brown. It is not available commercially as most of the stands of this tree were destroyed when scrubland was cleared for agriculture. Used for interior fixtures.

GENERAL NOTES: The Brown Pine is in general use as an ornamental tree; it is an evergreen with a dense crown of dark bluish-green foliage that provides excellent background for lighter-coloured plants. Other uses for it are in shelter belt planting and as a shade tree.

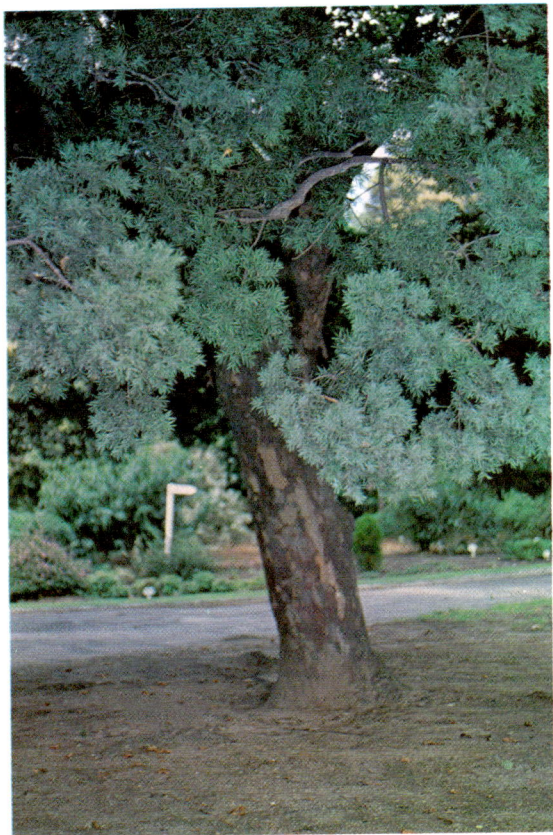

# BRUSH BOX

*Tristania conferta*                                      (Family Myrtaceae)

HABITAT: The coastal scrubs and forests from Port
Stephens, N.S.W., to Bowen, Queensland.

SIZE: Attains a height of 120 feet with a stem diameter of
up to 7 feet; seldom buttressed.

DESCRIPTION: Bark is brown or grey, scaly and variable,
sometimes very smooth in the upper branches. Young
leaves and shoots are covered with silky hairs. Leaves
are 5 inches long, alternate, from 3 to 5 crowded
together at ends of branchlets; they are elliptical and
taper at both ends; mid-rib and veins are prominent
on both sides with net-like veins; generally paler on
underside. Flowers are in small groups from 3 to 8
in the forks of the leaves or at the ends of branchlets;
one inch in diameter, with a bell-shaped calyx on which
5 small creamy-white petals are held. The ovary
consists of 3 cells.

TIMBER: Close-grained, hard and heavy but difficult to
season. It is used for general building purposes and is
an excellent flooring timber; colour is pinkish, dark
towards the centre. Is said to resist white ants.

GENERAL NOTES: Once the most extensively planted tree
in Australian suburban streets and parks. More
decorative and less vigorous trees have superseded it
but a variegated sport (cultivar) is, to a minor extent,
restoring its popularity. An excellent evergreen shade
tree, shapely and needing little attention, but does not
make a significant floral display. The blooms do,
however, supply apiarists with excellent honey.

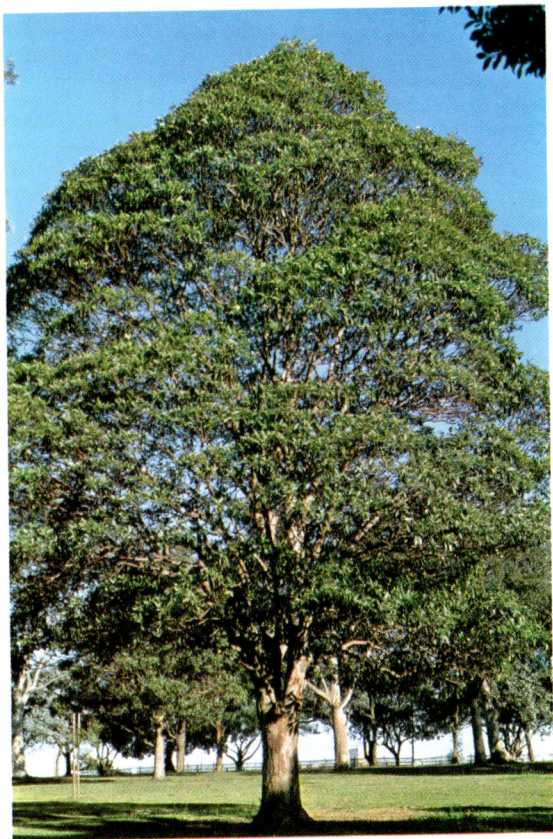

# BRUSH CHERRY

*Syzygium paniculatum* (Family Myrtaceae)

HABITAT: The coastal districts from Victoria to north Australia.

SIZE: An evergreen tree attaining a height of 60 feet with a stem diameter of 1 foot, occasionally slightly buttressed.

DESCRIPTION: Bark is brown and somewhat scaly. Leaves are 3 inches long, opposite, lance-shaped, with a short stalk, pointed at the apex and narrowing towards the base with mid-rib and veins prominent on both sides. Flowers are in panicles at the growing point of the branchlets or single in the leaf axils. The stamens are dense and prominent. Fruit is globular, $\frac{1}{2}$ inch in diameter, purplish-red and contains a single large seed surrounded by succulent pulp. The fruits are said to be edible.

TIMBER: Of little commercial value, sometimes used as scantling.

GENERAL NOTES: A fast-growing ornamental tree with shiny deep green foliage that is usually a rich burgundy at first. It is quite ornamental at flowering time but its main display is provided by its abundant berries which last for 8 weeks or longer during January/March. It is an excellent shade or shelter tree but is prone to scale insect attack which, unless checked, results in sooty mould discoloration. Previously referred to as *Eugenia australis* or *E. myrtifolia*, as well as Scrub Cherry.

# BUCKINGHAMIA

*Buckinghamia celsissima* (Family Proteaceae)

HABITAT: The rain forests of Queensland.

SIZE: Attains a height of 60 feet with a stem diameter up to 2 feet.

DESCRIPTION: Bark is dark grey, fine-textured and rough. Leaves are dark green, smooth, rather silky underneath, up to 8 inches long with prominent veins. They vary considerably, some are whole, either lanceolate or linear, while others are deeply divided or lobed into 3 or 5 segments. Flowers are in terminal clusters with individual spikes 4 to 8 inches long, like tapered cream-coloured bottlebrushes. Seed pods are 1 inch long capsules that split open on one side. Seeds are black, flat and surrounded by a narrow wing-like papery margin.

TIMBER: Close-grained with a beautiful figure; it takes a high polish; useful for cabinet work and turnery.

GENERAL NOTES: The Buckinghamia is becoming more popular as an ornamental tree. It is an evergreen with dense foliage, and regularly provides a splendid floral display for nearly four weeks during January and February, when it is completely covered with a silky mass of creamy, honey-laden blossoms.

# BUNYA PINE

*Araucaria bidwillii*              (Family Araucariaceae)

HABITAT: Found principally in the sheltered valleys of southern Queensland, mostly in the Bunya Mountains district and around Gympie. Needs rich soil and at least a 30 inch rainfall.

SIZE: Grows to 140 feet with a stem diameter from 3 to 5 feet; under forest conditions it attains a clean trunk of up to 80 feet to the first branch.

DESCRIPTION: Bark is thick and corky in horizontal scales. Foliage is very sharp; leaves have short leaf stalks, alternate, thick and crowded on the branchlets; narrow with a pungent point at the apex, glossy, dark green. Fruits are huge egg-shaped cones up to 12 inches in size, and heavy. Seeds are up to 2 inches in size, they were a favourite food of the Australian Aborigines. When the trees were in fruit it was a time of festivity and tribes would travel great distances to feast on the nuts which were roasted prior to eating.

TIMBER: Like Hoop Pine and put to similar uses.

GENERAL NOTES: The Bunya is a useful ornamental tree but it has lost popularity because of the sharp leaves which it sheds throughout the year. It is symmetrical, upright in growth and has a characteristic elliptical outline resembling the old-fashioned beehive. Branching is dense and clustered around the trunk like wheel spokes. The main stem persists to the top of the tree.

# CANDLE-BARK GUM

*Eucalyptus rubida*                    (Family Myrtaceae)

HABITAT: Victoria, the mountain ranges and colder districts of N.S.W. to the Queensland border; also in parts of S.A. and Tasmania.

SIZE: Grows to 100 feet with a stem diameter of up to 3 feet.

DESCRIPTION: Bark is smooth, buff coloured; shed in short rolled ribbons leaving a clean white stem that later changes to a rosy pink in the colder districts. Juvenile leaves are broad, pale grey. Mature leaves are alternate, pale green, narrow and smooth on both sides. Buds are in threes in the form of a cross (cruciform) in the axils of the leaves. Flowering is from January to February. The flowers are creamy white, on very short stalks. Capsules generally have a pale grey bloom; they are top-shaped or nearly hemispherical. Valves are triangular, either 3 or 4, exserted.

TIMBER: Has a pinkish tint, is hard, tough with open grain and is easy to work; used for general construction.

GENERAL NOTES: Extensively planted as an ornamental tree for parks and streets in areas of low rainfall and severe frosts. Develops a shapely dense crown when grown as a solitary specimen, but shows considerable variation in its habit of growth.

# CARBEEN

*Eucalyptus tesselaris* (Family Myrtaceae)

HABITAT: Eastern coast of Queensland and northern N.S.W., extends inland for 200 miles; the Gulf of Carpentaria; also Careening and Vansiltart Bays in W.A.; found mostly on the plains or on undulating country in sandy soils and fairly dry sites.

SIZE: Grows to a height of 100 feet with a 3 foot stem diameter.

DESCRIPTION: Bark is silvery-grey, smooth to the branch tips except for the base which is covered with black coarse bark that is deeply cracked into small rectangular segments. Leaves are alternate, on short stalks, dull greyish-green on both surfaces, venation not conspicuous. Flowers are in the leaf axils or in terminal panicles of two or four. Buds are pear-shaped on short stalks. Seed capsule is cylindrical, sometimes constricted in the middle.

TIMBER: Chocolate-brown, hard and tough with close grain; easy to work, dresses well, but is somewhat greasy; used mostly in structural and bridge work.

GENERAL NOTES: The Carbeen is a rather striking tree because of its smooth silvery upright stem and strongly-contrasted butt which is almost black in colour and rough textured. Bears a profusion of creamy honey-laden flowers from December to January which at times cover the tree completely. It is suitable for tropical forestry.

# CELERYWOOD

*Polyscias elegans*

(Family Araliaceae)

HABITAT: The coastal scrubs from southern N.S.W. to north Queensland, in sheltered valleys with good soil.

SIZE: Grows to 90 feet with a stem diameter of 2 feet.

DESCRIPTION: Bark is grey, coarsely wrinkled with a tesselated appearance. Leaves are large, up to 3 feet in older trees, pinnate or doubly pinnate; individual leaflets are opposite, on short stalks, egg-shaped with an abrupt sharp point, deep green and shiny, 3 inches long. Flowers are in great numbers on large terminal much-branched panicles, branchlets of which are clothed with minute hairs. The individual flowers are small, downy, on short stalks; ovary is 2 celled. Fruits are black, flattened discs less than $\frac{1}{4}$ inch diameter and contain 2 seeds.

TIMBER: Has no commercial value as it is soft, light and springy; it has been used for cricket bats and in musical instrument making.

GENERAL NOTES: The Celerywood is an excellent ornamental tree; it is globose in outline, evergreen, with shiny leaves that almost sparkle in the sun. The branches are well spaced and the pendant foliage has a graceful lacy appearance. It does best in areas where there is good soil and only mild frost. The flowers are rather inconspicuous but this is compensated by the dense cover of fruits which, in late autumn, give the tree an unusual 'smokey' appearance. Previously known as *Tieghemopanax elegans*.

# COAST CYPRESS PINE

*Callitris columellaris*                    (Family Cupressaceae)

HABITAT: Northern N.S.W. and southern Queensland coastal areas. Very numerous on Moreton and Bribie Islands as well as coastal areas of Queensland.

SIZE: Grows to a height of 60 feet with a stem diameter of 18 inches.

DESCRIPTION: Bark is dark-grey to black, rough, deeply fissured and contains tannin. Leaves are minute, angular, tightly clustered around the stem, greenish-blue in colour. The male flowers are arranged in cylindrical terminal clusters and the female flowers are on the lower branchlets. These develop into globular cones with 6 rough woody valves alternately large and small. Seeds are two-winged. Fruit cones persist for many years. Characteristic of this species is the triangular upright point (columella) in the centre of the cone which prompted the specific name.

TIMBER: Pale chocolate colour, easy to work, straight grained with attractive figure; aromatic and resists white ants. It has been used for cabinet making as it takes a high polish but as it is almost unobtainable in commercial quantities, is not well known.

GENERAL NOTES: Botanically, this tree is a true Conifer (Pine) although its cones bear little resemblance to the well-known pine tree cones. It is used extensively as a hedge plant and as a feature tree. The specimen pictured is growing in the Melbourne Botanic Gardens. Referred to in Queensland as Bribie Pine.

# COMMON PITTOSPORUM

*Pittosporum undulatum* (Family Pittosporaceae)

HABITAT: The eastern coast of Australia as far north as Gladstone, Queensland.

SIZE: Grows to 50 feet with a stem diameter of 1 foot.

DESCRIPTION: Bark is blackish-grey and smooth. Leaves are 3 inches long in groups of 3 to 6, those at the ends of branchlets almost whorled. They are lance-shaped, glossy, dark green with wavy margins. Flowers are compound clusters of creamy-white blooms, heavily scented with a perfume that somewhat resembles orange blossom; hence it is sometimes referred to as 'Mock Orange'. Fruit is a capsule with 2 hard thick leaves containing ruby-coloured seeds.

TIMBER: Known as White Hollywood; it is fine-textured, hard, ivory in colour with a close, straight grain; easy to work. Used to make draftsmen's scales, chessmen, wooden spoons and for carving.

GENERAL NOTES: A very popular evergreen tree in Australian parks and gardens; does well in almost all parts of the continent. It is globular in outline, makes a good specimen tree, and is used for hedge and shelter plantings. Branching is close and it provides dense shade. Unfortunately it is subject to white wax and other scales; cannot stand heavy frosts but will withstand moderate salt winds.

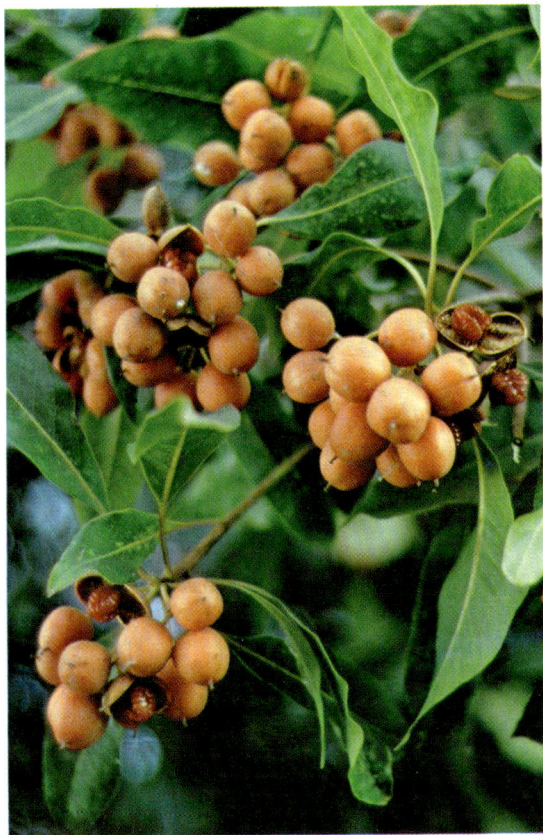

# COOTAMUNDRA WATTLE

*Acacia baileyana* (Family Leguminosae)

HABITAT: The districts of Cootamundra, Temora and Wagga Wagga in N.S.W.

SIZE: A small tree of up to 25 feet with a stem seldom above 1 foot in diameter.

DESCRIPTION: Bark is smooth, dark grey at the base of the stem, pale green on the branches. The leaves are bipinnate with numerous $\frac{1}{4}$ inch silvery leaflets crowded on 5 pairs of $1\frac{1}{2}$ inch long pinnae. Flowers are in short spikes, bright yellow balls on short stalks. The pods are pale green, flat, 2 inches long by $\frac{1}{2}$ inch wide.

TIMBER: In small sizes, only used as firewood.

GENERAL NOTES: Probably the commonest of the cultivated wattles. Very useful for interplanting as it is short-lived, seldom surviving after ten years, during the last three of which it generally becomes borer infested. Extremely hardy, fast growing and dense as well as low branching and therefore ideal for rapidly establishing a windbreak. Very colourful when in flower in early spring and decorative for the rest of the year.

# COTTONTREE HIBISCUS

*Hibiscus tiliaceus*         (Family Malvaceae)

HABITAT: Coastal strip of northern N.S.W., Queensland and the islands of the Pacific. It is quite often found in swampy situations.

SIZE: Grows to 30 feet with a stem diameter of one foot; globular in outline; stem is seldom upright.

DESCRIPTION: Bark is pale grey, fairly smooth; the fibres are little affected by moisture and were used by the Aborigines for making fishing nets and fishing lines. Leaves are heart-shaped (round cordate), smooth on the upper side and slightly hairy and white underneath, up to 5 inches in diameter with long slender stalks. Flowers are 3 inches across, cadmium-yellow with a crimson throat, 5 petals with the typical Mallow structure, the stamens united around a central column (style) with 5 discs. Seed capsules are one inch long with 5 cells containing small smooth brown hard seeds.

TIMBER: Close-grained, somewhat greenish, well-marked, easy to work and takes a polish. It is sought after by boat builders for 'knees'.

GENERAL NOTES: The Cottontree Hibiscus (Cottonwood in Queensland) is a fast-growing evergreen tree useful for ornamental plantings in difficult situations. It can thrive in soil that is occasionally flooded. Develops into a shapely round-headed tree, densely branched and thickly foliaged; it bears a profusion of large yellow flowers throughout the summer. Growth is often rampant but it can be pruned in late winter.

# DAVIDSON'S PLUM

*Davidsonia pruriens*          (Family Davidsoniaceae)

HABITAT: The sub-tropical and tropical rain forests of northern N.S.W. and eastern Queensland in areas of deep soil and plentiful rainfall.

SIZE: Height is up to 40 feet with a stem diameter of 1 foot.

DESCRIPTION: Bark is smooth, dark grey, sometimes with horizontal rings. Leaves are pinnate, 2 to 3 feet long, the stalk bordered with short pointed lobes; individual leaflets are up to 1 foot long by 3 inches broad, with serrated edges and short stalks. The young shoots are covered with sharp hairs. Flowers are in 1 foot long pendant panicles, clustered around short branches; the calyx is red and consists of 2 small lobes; the petals are absent; there are 8 to 10 stamens and 2 styles. Fruit is a 3 inch purple berry that has a loose covering of short brown hairs; the pulpy, bitter red flesh encloses 2 flat seeds.

TIMBER: Dark brown, close-grained, tough and durable; has been used for tool handles and mallets.

GENERAL NOTES: The columnar habit of this tree makes it ideal as a focal point for special effects. It usually has several vertical stems from which the large leaves hang gracefully in an irregular pattern. The fruits are clustered under the topmost leaves. They are used for jams and jellies. Flying foxes relish them.

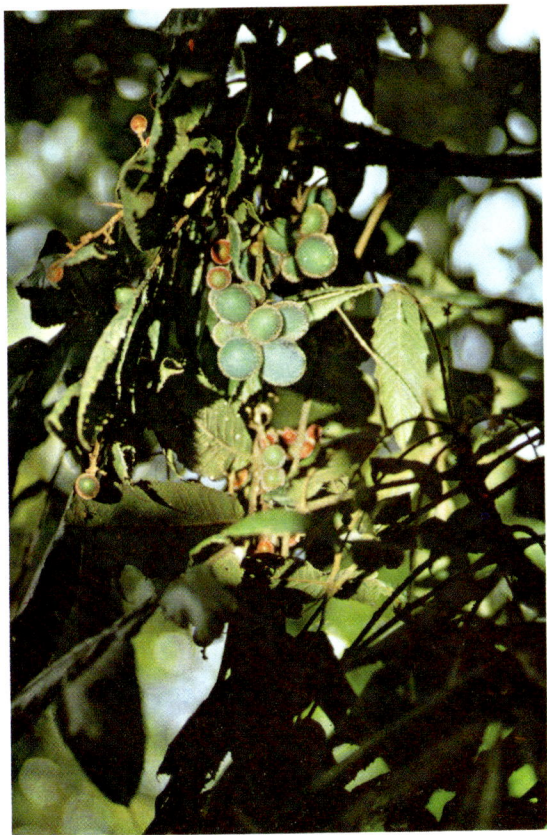

# DIAMOND-LEAVED PITTOSPORUM

*Pittosporum rhombifolium* (Family Pittosporaceae)

HABITAT: The coastal jungles of Queensland where it grows as scattered specimens among Eucalypts or rain forest trees.

SIZE: In forest gullies it reaches to 60 feet with a stem diameter of 14 inches but it is seldom higher than 20 feet when grown as a solitary specimen.

DESCRIPTION: Bark is smooth, dark grey and is persistent (not shed). Leaves are almost diamond shaped, a glossy, dark green, 3 inches long and irregularly toothed from halfway to tip. Flowers are in terminal clusters, white, small but numerous. Capsules are bright orange, almost pear-shaped and contain 2 or 3 sticky black seeds.

TIMBER: Ivory-white, fine-textured with little grain, develops a good sheen, tough but easy to work. Used for chessmen, draughtsman's scales and turnery.

GENERAL NOTES: Used a great deal as a small ornamental tree or as a decorative evergreen hedge plant. Very showy for several weeks during late summer, when it is regularly covered with orange 'berries'. Birds are enticed by the small black seeds which later germinate readily in nearby gardens.

# DROOPING SHEOAK

*Casuarina stricta*                    (Family Casuarinaceae)

HABITAT: Every state except Queensland, both on the coast and inland, on most types of soils in association with a variety of other trees.

SIZE: Seldom more than 20 feet, often shrubby.

DESCRIPTION: Better described as a leafless tree as the leaves are reduced to small scales arranged in whorls around the branchlets which carry out the function of leaves. Male and female flowers are on different trees; the male or pollen-bearing flowers are brownish-pink in dense terminal catkin-like spikes, 2 to 4 inches long by $\frac{1}{4}$ inch in diameter; the female flowers are in tight clusters on older branchlets; they later form a globular woody cone 1 to 2 inches in diameter. The seeds are tiny brown 'nuts' with a papery wing.

TIMBER: Red with prominent darker bands, takes a high polish. Has been used for axe handles, staves, spokes and in turnery. Makes excellent firewood leaving little or no ash.

GENERAL NOTES: Can thrive in some of the most exposed situations on dry, stony ridges where there are strong winds and hard frosts. Native stands are being destroyed by grazing as it is an excellent fodder plant. The male plants are drooping in habit, the name *stricta*, meaning upright, is more applicable to the female tree. Often referred to as Mountain Oak.

# FLAME TREE

*Brachychiton acerifolium*  (Family Sterculiaceae)

HABITAT: The coastal scrubs from Illawarra, N.S.W., to north Queensland.

SIZE: A large tree sometimes attaining a height of 100 feet with a stem diameter of 3 feet, generally cylindrical.

DESCRIPTION: Upright habit of growth with the stem generally persisting to the tip of the tree. Bark is grey or brownish, prominently fissured, up to 2 inches in thickness and furnishes a lace-like fibre that has been used for rope, mat and hat making. Branchlets, leaves and flowers are hairless. Leaf stalks are long, slender, 3 to 9 inches long. Leaves alternate, 10 inches across, quite variable in shape, with 3 lobes or deeply divided. The flowers are in large and conspicuous panicles up to 7 inches in length in the forks of the upper leaves. The bell-shaped red calyx forms the flower with 5 lobes on its rim. Male and female flowers are sometimes on the same tree. Fruit is a 3 to 5 inch long, boat-shaped follicle.

TIMBER: Wood is soft, light in weight, and has no commercial value.

GENERAL NOTES: Flame Tree is an apt name as it is brilliant when in full bloom. Forest trees are most conspicuous when they are in flower, in December/January. As a garden or park tree, it has few rivals in popularity but it needs deep rich soil and ample moisture. Growth is unpredictable and flowering is often patchy; about every third year it defoliates completely and then makes an excellent colour·display.

# GREY MANGROVE

*Avicennia marina* (Family Avicenniaceae)

HABITAT: Grows on the Australian sea coast except Tasmania; it is usually found in thick stands or occasionally as a conspicuous solitary specimen towering above the lower-growing river mangroves (*Aegiceras corniculatum*).

SIZE: Grows to 40 feet with a stem diameter of 18 inches.

DESCRIPTION: Bark is light grey, smooth and thin. Leaves are opposite, thick, lanceolate or broad lanceolate, 3 inches long, pointed, short stalk; the underside of the leaves is silvery-white, covered with short silky hairs. Flowers are yellow to orange in clusters or small heads, on rigid angular stalks in the axils of the leaves, at the ends of the branches. Individual flowers are small, $\frac{1}{8}$ inch, with 5 sepals and short corollary tube, 4 stamens and one-celled ovary. Honey produced from these has a strong flavour. The fruit is a small capsule with a solitary seed which germinates inside the fruit before it drops off (as a rule vertically), thereby giving the young plant an opportunity of developing in the tidal mud in which the tree normally grows.

TIMBER: Pale-coloured, strong, hard, durable, heavy and cross-laminated like a 5 ply veneer.

GENERAL NOTES: The Grey Mangrove is a very useful tree for planting along tidal rivers or foreshores. Its roots develop peg-like projections above the surface of the mud around the tree through which air is absorbed at low tide.

# HOOP PINE

*Araucaria cunninghamii*        (Family Araucariaceae)

HABITAT: The east coast of Australia from northern
N.S.W. to New Guinea, sometimes up to 100 miles
inland. Grows from sea level to 2500 feet in areas of
deep soil, with at least a 30 inch rainfall.

SIZE: Grows to 150 feet with a stem diameter of up to
5 feet. In forests it sometimes attains a clean stem up
to 90 feet; the stem is persistent to the top of the tree.

DESCRIPTION: Bark is rough, close-textured, scaly, in
horizontal bands or hoops. Leaves are narrow and
triangular in shape, 4 inches long and sharp. Fruits
are circular cones that disintegrate when the seeds are
ripe.

TIMBER: Sometimes referred to as Queensland Pine,
Colonial Pine, Dorrigo or Richmond River Pine, it is
of exceptional value for case making, indoor fittings
and flooring, and comprises the bulk of plywood and
veneer board in the Queensland trade. Due to its
commercial value native stands have been practically
cut out; however, the Queensland Forestry Department
is replanting extensive acreages.

GENERAL NOTES: The Hoop Pine is a graceful evergreen,
conical tree. Its great height makes it ideal for creating
a strong vertical accent in a large landscape composi-
tion. From seed it shows marked variation in form;
a characteristic that becomes very evident when it is
used for avenue planting. Foliage is deep green but a
glaucous (bluish) variety grows around Rockhampton
and the Whitsunday Passage.

# KURRAJONG

*Brachychiton populneum*                (Family Sterculiaceae)

HABITAT: A widely-distributed scrub tree found in Victoria, on the western plains of N.S.W. and up into Queensland, particularly on rocky limestone ridges.

SIZE: Attains a height of 50 feet with a stem diameter of 2 feet, stem is sometimes swollen at the base.

DESCRIPTION: Bark is grey, vertically furrowed, hard and thick. The young shoots, leaves and flowers are covered with soft hairs. Leaves are most variable, alternate, 3 to 7 lobed, 4 to 8 inches in diameter, pale and hairy on the underside. Young leaves are deeply divided into lobes. Flowers are arranged in narrow panicles at the ends of the branches, they are bell-shaped, about $\frac{3}{4}$ inch long, greenish in colour with brown markings inside and are laden with nectar that is sought by bees.

Fruit is a 3 to 5 lobed follicle, 4 inches long, boat-shaped, generally in a cluster, open at one side and containing up to 30 oval seeds $\frac{1}{2}$ inch long. Each seed covered with a papery wall and all are tightly packed in the follicle. The inside of the carpel is covered with stiff brown hairs. Flowers December to March.

TIMBER: Wood is soft and has no commercial value.

GENERAL NOTES: The Kurrajong is a very popular tree with land owners; many use it as a fodder plant as well as for shade and shelter plantings. It is one of the few evergreen native trees that transplants success-fully when quite large.

# LEMON IRONWOOD

*Backhousia citriodora* (Family Myrtaceae)

HABITAT: The north coast of N.S.W. and as far as Mackay, Queensland, in the mixed jungles of coastal watersheds.

SIZE: Grows to 40 feet with a stem diameter of 1 foot, often without branches for two-thirds of its height.

DESCRIPTION: Bark is thin, fissured, dark grey. The young shoots are hairy. Leaves are opposite, 2 to 4 inches long, with short stalks and entire or slightly toothed margins, the underside often paler and downy. They have a strong citron smell when crushed. The flowers are in clusters in the leaf axils at the ends of the branches; they are borne in profusion and resemble gum blooms. The calyx lobes persist and expand forming a two-celled fruit.

TIMBER: Very hard, straight-grained, pink or red with little sapwood; has been used for mallets and turnery.

GENERAL NOTES: The Lemon Ironwood or as it is sometimes called, the Sweet Verbena tree, is an evergreen that is most attractive at flowering time when it is completely covered with creamy flowers. These are honey-laden and attract insects including the highly-coloured Jewel Beetles. When grown as an ornamental tree, it tends to remain shrub-like with multiple stems that form into a dense shapely crown. The foliage is ornamental and its citron scent is most refreshing.

# LEMON-SCENTED GUM

*Eucalyptus citriodora* (Family Myrtaceae)

HABITAT: Central and northern Queensland, where it grows in undulating country on a variety of soils including poor soil; generally associated with White Mahogany (*E. triantha*), Grey Gum (*E. propinqua*) and Narrow-Leafed Ironbark (*E. crebra*).

SIZE: Grows to a height of 120 feet with a stem diameter up to 4 feet; has a clean straight stem.

DESCRIPTION: Bark is white with a smooth, powdery surface, and is shed in thin scales. Leaves are alternate, narrowly lanceolate, 6 inches long and are pale green on both sides; venation not conspicuous. A commercial oil (Citronella) used in perfumery is obtained from the leaves. Flowers are terminal in groups of 3 on short stalks. Seed cups are ovoid.

TIMBER: Light brown, hard, tough; grain is straight or interlocked, sometimes wavy or with fiddle-back figure, somewhat greasy. Used for heavy framing where hardness and shock-resistance are required.

GENERAL NOTES: The colour of the bark is lighter on trees growing in the south than in the north of the continent. The Lemon-Scented Gum was one of the first gums to be used for ornamental purposes, probably because of its very strong, refreshing citronella odour. When planted as a solitary specimen, the branching tends to start lower down the stem, usually developing into a well-shaped tree with a ghost-like white trunk and branches.

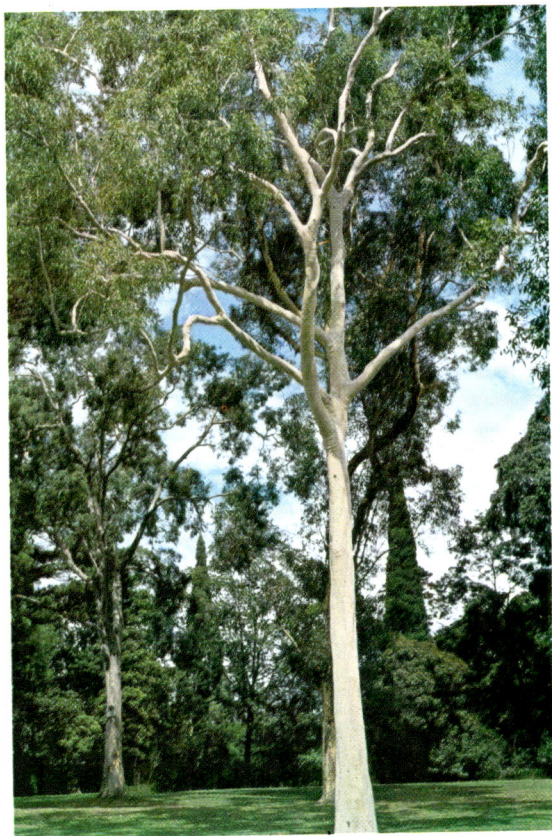

# MORETON BAY FIG

*Ficus macrophylla*                    (Family Moraceae)

HABITAT: The east coast of Australia from southern N.S.W. to north Queensland.

SIZE: Attains a height of 160 feet and in common with many rain forest trees, has a deeply-buttressed stem.

DESCRIPTION: Bark exudes the typical viscous milky sap that, in one species (*F. elastica*) was an early source of rubber. Leaves are glossy green, pale on the underside, from 6 to 10 inches long, with a one-inch stalk. The leaf buds are pointed, upright, and protected by stipules that vary in colour from white to deep pink. Fruit is a one-inch diameter globular fig, purple with white dots when ripe, often borne in great profusion; it is sought by flying foxes; both fruit and leaves are eaten by cattle.

GENERAL NOTES: This tree usually starts life from seed that germinates in leaf mould, high up in the forks of other trees, then sending roots down to ground level. Once these reach the soil they quickly develop and eventually form a tree trunk that smothers the host tree. The Moreton Bay Fig was once very popular as a shade tree, especially in streets where it gave dense shade to horse-drawn transport. Nowadays its roots are considered to be too invasive. When grown in the open it develops into a magnificent, symmetrical tree that is unrivalled as a solitary specimen.

# MOUNTAIN ASH

*Eucalyptus regnans*         (Family Myrtaceae)

HABITAT: Tasmania, eastern and southern Victoria in moist mountain valleys with deep rich soil; generally in pure stands.

SIZE: One of the largest of the gums, 200 to 300 feet tall, with a stem diameter of up to 9 feet.

DESCRIPTION: Stems are vertical shafts sometimes over 100 feet to the first branch. Bark is creamy or grey, smooth, fibrous at the stem base for up to 30 feet; shed in long ribbons. Juvenile leaves are opposite, mature leaves are alternate, narrow and curved with distinct veins, glossy on both sides and with numerous transparent oil dots. Flowers are in the axils of the leaves, ivory white, small, solitary or in pairs. Flowering time is between January and March. Capsules are stalked, small and semi-ovate; covered with white waxy bloom; the valves are enclosed.

TIMBER: Referred to in the trade as Australian Oak; light with straight grain; pale brown; in great demand for building construction, also used for furniture.

GENERAL NOTES: Tallest of the Australian trees with records of exceptional trees 322 and 375 feet tall. It is an important timber tree. Also known as Giant Gum and in Tasmania as Swamp Gum. A forest of these trees is one of the truly impressive sights of the Australian bush.

# MOUNTAIN EBONY

*Bauhinia hookeri* (Family Leguminosae)

HABITAT: Central Queensland and dry coastal areas up to Torres Strait.

SIZE: Grows to 50 feet with a stem diameter of 2 feet; forms a large spreading crown.

DESCRIPTION: Bark is dark grey, hard and fissured vertically. Leaves are simple and two-lobed, folding along the mid-rib with each half closing up face-to-face under adverse conditions; mid-green in colour, slightly paler underneath, smooth, with 5 to 7 radiating veins fairly prominent, 1 inch overall. Flowers have 5 petals $1\frac{1}{2}$ inches long, white, edged pink, on short-stalked terminal racemes. Pod is sickle-shaped, 4 inches long, flat, 1 inch broad with 2 to 4 seeds.

TIMBER: Dark brown, beautifully marked, close-grained, hard, heavy, and suitable for cabinet work.

GENERAL NOTES: Although not quite as spectacular as the exotic Bauhinias, the Mountain Ebony is a delicately beautiful tree when in full bloom. It has been used for ornamental plantings in the warmer zones of Australia but growth is slow even under excellent conditions. Branches are large and well spaced; foliage is evergreen, often with a deep pink hue when young. The outline is rounded; sometimes develops multiple stems when grown in the open.

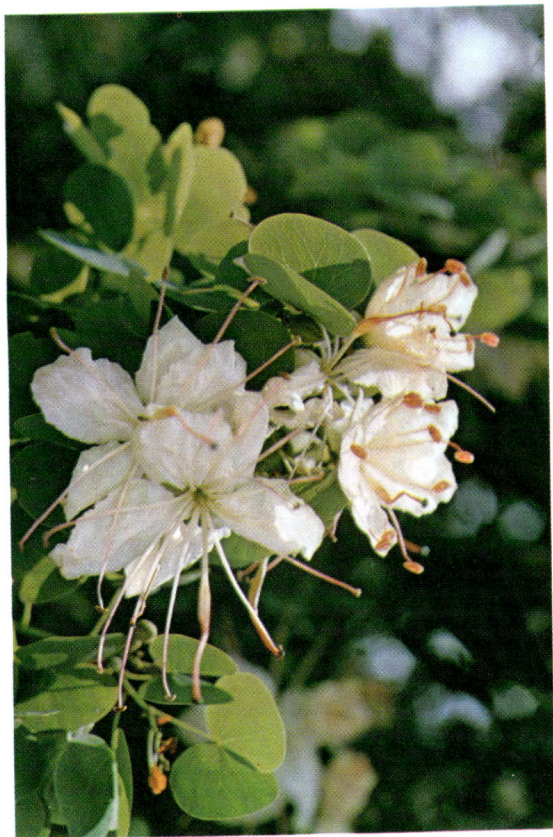

# NATIVE FRANGIPANNI

*Hymenosporum flavum*                    (Family Pittosporaceae)

HABITAT: East coast of Australia, generally in association with rain forests.

SIZE: Grows to 60 feet with a one foot stem diameter.

DESCRIPTION: Bark is closely pitted, smooth and pale grey. Leaves are alternate, oblong, smooth, dark green, up to 5 inches long with short stalks. Flowers are in loose panicles, the individual flower is tubular, 1 inch long, deep yellow changing to cream as it ages, hairy on the outside. Fruit is a flattened capsule 2 inches long by 1 inch broad and contains flat, papery, glossy brown-winged seeds stacked in laminated layers.

TIMBER: Is without sapwood, whitish, close-grained and tough; it is easy to work and suitable for cabinet work.

GENERAL NOTES: This evergreen tree is usually grown from seed; it makes fast growth but is unpredicatable in its flowering habit; good specimens can be a mass of flowers in spring but quite often the branching is so sparse that the floral display is disappointing. In cultivation it seldom exceeds 25 feet in height; its slender stem, irregular outline and colourful, sweetly scented flowers have made it a favourite in home gardens.

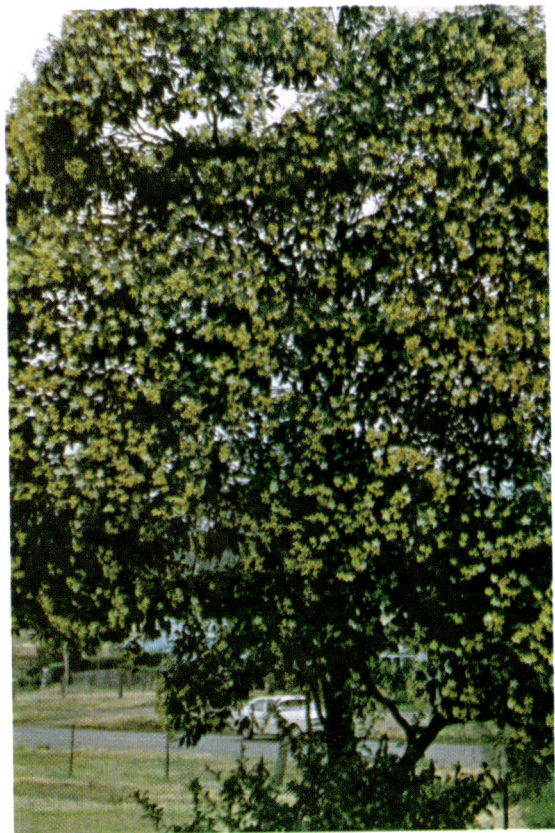

# NATIVE OLIVE

*Notelaea microcarpa*         (Family Oleaceae)

HABITAT: The western plains of N.S.W. and as far north as Rockhampton, Queensland, in open forest and areas of low rainfall.

SIZE: Grows to 30 feet with a stem diameter of 1 foot but is generally smaller.

DESCRIPTION: Branches are slender and crowded, smooth, often whitish at the tips. Bark is blackish-grey, coarse and persistent. Leaves are narrow, lanceolate, from 3 to 5 inches long, 1 inch wide, tapering to a point; dark green, veins prominent on the upper surface. Flowers are tiny, in the axils of the leaves. Fruit is $\frac{1}{4}$ to $\frac{1}{2}$ inch in diameter, white or purplish and contains a single seed.

TIMBER: Light coloured, close-grained and hard, not available in commercial sizes.

GENERAL NOTES: This is one of a small genus of Australian trees that is relatively unknown in cultivation. It does, however, deserve more attention, particularly for dry areas where it will thrive in poor soil, under conditions of drought, intense summer heat and severe winter frost. It has some value as a fodder tree.

# PORT JACKSON FIG

*Ficus rubiginosa*                    (Family Moraceae)

HABITAT: The coast of N.S.W. and as far inland as Narrabri.

SIZE: Grows to 100 feet with a stem diameter of 6 feet.

DESCRIPTION: Stem is buttress-like at the base. It is a smaller tree than the Moreton Bay Fig, has smaller leaves and denser branching. Bark is pale grey and smooth. Leaves are egg-shaped or elliptical, 4 to 5 inches long, usually with rusty-coloured hairs on the underside; leaf stalks are often hairy. Fruits are small figs similar to the edible fig (*Ficus carica*), $\frac{1}{2}$ inch in diameter, borne in the leaf axils, either singly or in pairs; they were used for food by the Port Jackson Aborigines. The root fibre is very durable and was used by the Aborigines in making fishing nets.

TIMBER: Soft, brittle, spongy, but has been used for packing cases.

GENERAL NOTES: It was once used extensively as an evergreen ornamental tree for gardens and streets but a smaller sized variegated form has superseded it in popularity. The fruits and leaves are regarded as excellent fodder for cattle and horses.

# PRICKLY PAPERBARK

*Melaleuca styphelioides* (Family Myrtaceae)

HABITAT: Victoria and southern N.S.W. usually in damp places and along water courses.

SIZE: A small compact tree seldom over 40 feet in height with a stem diameter of up to 2 feet.

DESCRIPTION: Bark is creamy white and peels off in papery layers. Leaves are alternate, rigid, ½ inch long and sharply pointed. Flowers are in cylindrical, bottle-brush spikes at the tips of the branches which continue their growth before the flower is spent. Numerous and closely-packed woody seed capsules.

TIMBER: Reddish-brown, straight-grained, very durable in waterlogged ground; partially resistant to the *Teredo* borer. Used in cabinet work, gunstocks, bridge-work, also for fencing and in jetty construction.

GENERAL NOTES: Forms into a well-shaped evergreen tree when grown as a solitary specimen; it often develops multiple stems. There are several excellent specimens in the Melbourne Botanic Gardens. Useful for shade or shelter in wet or saline soils. The bark is used for lining hanging baskets and the stems are regarded as ideal for growing and displaying various epiphytes. Also known as Prickly-leaved Tea-tree.

# QUEENSLAND KAURI

*Agathis robusta*             (Family Araucariaceae)

HABITAT: The coastal regions of south Queensland from sea level to 3,000 feet elevation in areas of good soil and high rainfall.

SIZE: It grows to 150 feet, the cylindrical bole often branchless up to 100 feet; stem diameter is from 3 to 4 feet but occasionally 10 feet. The branching at the top of the tree forms an abrupt change from the tall columnar stem.

DESCRIPTION: Bark in older trees becomes scaly but is smooth in young trees. Leaves are opposite, 3 to 4 inches long and 1 inch in breadth, and show little leaf stalk; they are elliptical in outline, dark green with slightly paler undersurface; indistinct veins. Male and female cones are usually borne on the same tree. Seeds are $\frac{1}{2}$ inch long and winged on one side.

TIMBER: Pale cream, easy to work, stains well and is used for cabinet work, shelving and indoor fittings. It was extensively used for butter box making as it did not taint and up to $1\frac{1}{2}$ million Kauri butter boxes were exported annually. The demand for this timber was such that most of the native stands have been felled and the remaining trees are carefully preserved for seed production only.

GENERAL NOTES: A forest giant well suited for bold effects or as a strong accent in large-scale landscape plantings.

# QUEENSLAND NUT

*Macadamia integrifolia*
(Family Proteaceae)

HABITAT: The scrub forests of the Australian east coast from Camdenhaven, N.S.W. to Maryborough, Queensland.

SIZE: Under forest conditions grows to 60 feet with a 1 foot diameter stem, but when grown in the open or under orchard conditions, develops as a dense-branching smaller tree.

DESCRIPTION: Bark is dark grey and smooth. Leaves, about 9 inches long by $1\frac{1}{2}$ inches broad, are arranged on the branchlets in whorls; they are rigid, long and narrow with undulating margins, sometimes entire and other times with spiny serrations; veins are conspicuous on both surfaces. The flowers hang from the axils of the leaves in 10 inch racemes; they are cream-coloured and after fertilization develop globular green fruits an inch or more in diameter; the outer skin splits to release the nut. The kernel is regarded as one of the best flavoured nuts of commerce.

GENERAL NOTES: It is a shapely evergreen well suited for ornamental use in streets or small gardens. It should, however, be given a deep rich soil. As a rule, fruit is seldom produced before the tree is seven years old. This tree is grown extensively in Hawaii where 'paper shell' varieties have been developed—a much-needed improvement as the wild varieties have an extremely hard shell.

# RED CEDAR

*Toona australis*                        (Family Meliaceae)

HABITAT: From Illawarra, N.S.W., to Queensland, more particularly in the warmer and moister regions, also India and Asia.

SIZE: Grows to 200 feet; stem diameter up to 10 feet.

DESCRIPTION: Bark is scaly and flakes off leaving a smooth reddish-brown trunk; fibrous and will tear off in layers. Leaves are alternate, pinnate with 3 to 8 pairs of leaflets, each 3 inches long. Flowers are large panicles of small $\frac{1}{4}$ inch blooms, with a fragrant honey scent. Fruit is a delicate, small dry capsule that splits into 5 valves containing thin winged seeds.

TIMBER: Most valuable, equal to mahogany which it somewhat resembles, but lighter in weight and with a pleasant odour; very durable and beautifully figured. It is rarely attacked by white ants. Used for tables, cabinets, furniture and interior fittings. Few timbers can surpass it in beauty of colour, which is a pleasing red turning richer with age.

GENERAL NOTES: Because of its commercial value, the Red Cedar was much sought after in the early days of colonization and timber-getters opened up large areas of new land in their search of this tree. It is seldom grown as an ornamental as it needs excellent conditions; given these it rapidly develops a columnar stem and a rather sparse crown. The Red Cedar Tip Moth (*Hypsiphyla robusta*) often damages forest plantations of this tree.

# RIVER OAK

*Casuarina cunninghamiana* (Family Casuarinaceae)

HABITAT: The east coast of Australia from southern
N.S.W. to north Queensland and the northern portion
of the Northern Territory. Almost invariably in pure
stands along watercourses.

SIZE: Maximum size is 100 feet tall with a stem diameter
of 4 feet. Average height is 80 feet with a diameter of
2 feet.

DESCRIPTION: Columnar stem, sometimes to the tip of
the tree. Bark is hard, dark grey, persistent and is
closely fissured vertically. Leaves are tiny, arranged
in whorls around the branchlets which act as leaves
(cladodes). The male and female flowers are on
separate trees; the male flowers are rusty-red in whorls
at the tips of the branchlets; the female flowers are
in tiny pink whorls that later develop into one-inch
cones, often arranged in groups around a branch.

TIMBER: Dark brown, hard and durable, with an oak-
like grain that gave rise to its common name. Used
for tool handles, cask staves, fancy turnery and
shingles; prized as bakers' wood.

GENERAL NOTES: Develops into a well-shaped columnar
tree when grown as a solitary specimen. It has been
used in streets and parks as an ornamental shade
tree, the male tree turning a reddish brown at flowering
time. It is frost-hardy, makes rapid growth and its
evergreen foliage makes a useful fodder reserve in
drought times.

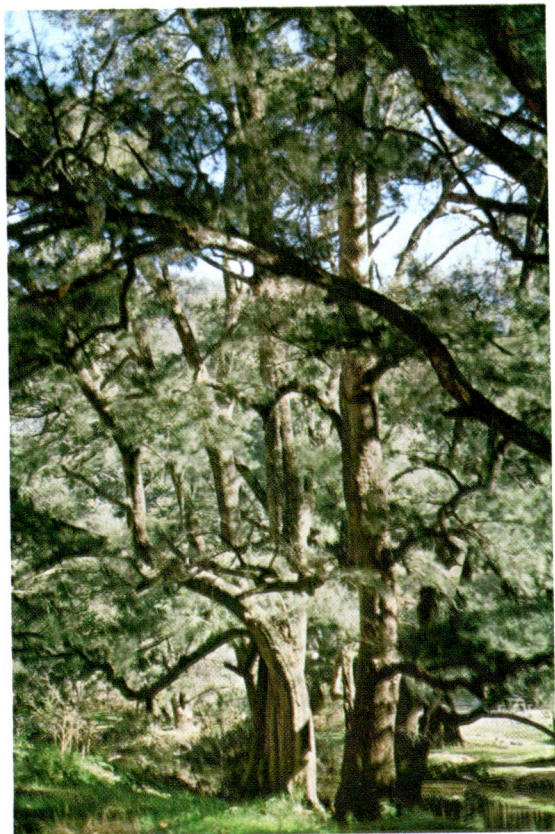

# RIVER RED GUM

*Eucalyptus camaldulensis*                   (Family Myrtaceae)

HABITAT: From South Australia to the Northern
  Territory and in the north-western part of W.A.,
  mostly on river flats and flood plains.

SIZE: Reaches up to 120 feet with a stem diameter of
  up to 6 feet, sometimes with a clean, vertical stem
  and rounded crown; at other times squat.

DESCRIPTION: The bark is smooth, light brown or grey,
  flakes off in large strips but is often retained around
  the base. The adult leaves are up to 10 inches long by
  one inch wide, smooth on both sides, pale green; they
  have a prominent intra-marginal vein, venation is at
  45 degrees. Flowers are in the leaf axils in small
  clusters of 5 to 10, on slender, short stalks; they contain sweet honey; Seed capsules are woody, globose,
  with incurved valves.

TIMBER: Dense with strong grain, red colour; durable,
  white-ant resistant; used in buildings and bridge work
  where large size and strength are essential.

GENERAL NOTES: It is the most widespread of the gums.
  A most picturesque tree along the banks of the
  Murray and Condamine Rivers where its growth is
  sometimes stunted. By contrast it is a shapely giant in
  savannah woodland where it may grow in association
  with Yellow Box (*E. melliodora*), Black Box (*E. bicolor*)
  and Grey Box (*E. microcarpa*).

# SATINWOOD

*Premna lignum-vitae*                                    (Family Verbenaceae)

HABITAT: Northern N.S.W. and south-eastern Queensland, generally in deep alluvial loams.

SIZE: Grows to 130 feet with a stem diameter of 3 feet.

DESCRIPTION: Branches are slender, crowded; the tips of the young branchlets are downy with rust-coloured hairs. Bark is yellowish-grey, rough and often finely fissured or ribbed. Leaves are opposite, 4 inches long, elliptical, sometimes lobed, pointed at the apex, glossy above, with mid-rib and veins more prominent underneath. Flowers are in small clusters in the axils of the leaves, cup-shaped at the base with tubular purple petals widening into 4 lobes. The fruit is a globular red berry about $\frac{3}{4}$ inch in diameter, it contains a round pip enclosing from 1 to 4 seeds.

TIMBER: Yellow in colour, called Yellow Hollywood in the timber trade; available in limited quantities; hard with a slightly oily surface, sometimes with fiddleback grain. Used for carving, engraving, tool handles, turnery, also in flooring and for fencing as it is durable in the ground.

GENERAL NOTES: Seldom grown as an ornamental but it is quite decorative. An excellent specimen is growing near the North Terrace entrance of the Adelaide Botanic Gardens. Fruits are produced irregularly; when ripe they make an attractive carpet around the base of the tree. Generally develops a somewhat columnar crown of dense evergreen foliage. Previously known as *Vitex lignum-vitae*.

# SILKY OAK

*Grevillea robusta*

(Family Proteaceae)

HABITAT: Eastern Australia where it is found in rain forests and occasionally in open forest.

SIZE: Grows to 120 feet with a stem diameter of 3 feet.

DESCRIPTION: Growth is upright with the stem persisting to the tip of the tree. Bark is dark grey, much furrowed by fissures. The leaves are alternate, double pinnate, individual leaflets are 1 inch long, lanceolate, sometimes divided at the apex; smooth, deep green upper surface and silvery grey underneath. Flowers are panicles of orange-coloured blooms, the individual flowers having the typical Proteaceous features. Base of style develops into a woody follicle containing one or two thin papery seeds.

TIMBER: Light pink with a silky lustre and an English Oak figure; soft but tough, durable, and carves well; it is a good veneer and one of the finest cabinet timbers. Together with *Orites excelsa*, it was for many years the commercial source of Silky Oak timber, but when the supply ran out *Carwellia sublimis* was substituted, and most of today's silky oak is from this tree.

GENERAL NOTES: This is probably the most commonly grown street tree in country towns throughout N.S.W. It is almost evergreen, columnar, has fern-like foliage and is strikingly colourful at flowering time, generally for 3 weeks in October or November.

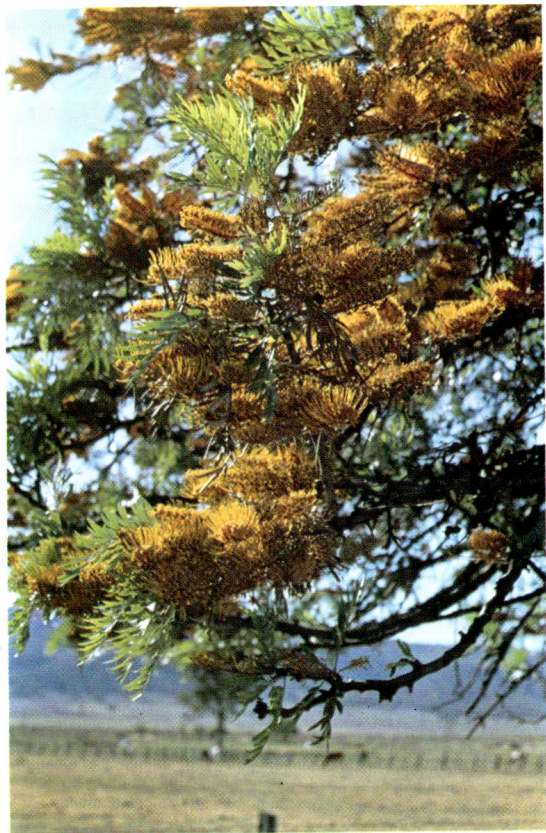

# SMALL-LEAF LILLY-PILLY

*Syzygium luehmannii* (Family Myrtaceae)

HABITAT: From the Richmond River, N.S.W., to Cairns, Q., in areas of good rainfall, generally along the watercourses of scrubs and rain forest.

SIZE: Will grow to 80 feet and up to 3 feet in diameter but is generally much smaller.

DESCRIPTION: The stem in large trees is often buttressed at the base. Bark is dark grey, smooth and persistent. Leaves are opposite, 2 inches long, 1 inch broad, smooth, dark green, and pointed at the apex; young leaves are yellowish to bright pink. Flowers are in terminal clusters in the axils of the leaves at the ends of the branchlets; cream-coloured with 4 or 5 minute petals and numerous stamens. The fruit is $\frac{1}{2}$ inch long, ovoid, or pear-shaped, bright red. The single seed is surrounded by acidulous pulp.

TIMBER: Bright red, light and tough, with little figure; has fine, straight grain; takes stain and polishes well. Used in fancy turnery, for mouldings and as flooring.

GENERAL NOTES: Very popular as an evergreen ornamental tree. As a solitary specimen it forms into a dense, fine textured, shapely tree. In good seasons or under garden conditions it produces several flushes of bright pink foliage throughout the year. Some trees are heavy croppers but others are shy bearers and fail to produce the additional display provided by the attractive red fruits. Previously known as *Eugenia luehmannii*.

# SMOOTH BARK APPLE

*Angophora costata* (Family Myrtaceae)

HABITAT: From the coastal districts and mountain ranges of N.S.W. to Rockhampton and central Queensland. Found mostly in rocky ground and attains a great size under what appear to be harsh conditions.

SIZE: Grows up to 100 feet with a stem diameter of 3 feet.

DESCRIPTION: Bark has a uniform pinkish-red colour; often stained with Kino which is exuded in considerable quantity and is sometimes gathered for use in the manufacture of astringents. Base of the tree will at times flatten out and spread over rocks, producing a most unusual effect as if the base of the tree stem had at some time softened and sagged. Leaves are opposite, lanceolate, 4 inches long, red when young, bright green later; venation is parallel. Flowers are clustered in terminal corymbs and resemble creamy gum tree blossoms. Fruits are small, ovoid, woody seed cups.

TIMBER: Usually has gum veins; used for flooring boards and fuel.

GENERAL NOTES: The Smooth Bark Apple grows into a majestic tree with a clean columnar stem and a dense spreading head of angular branches. A stand of mature trees is an impressive sight, particularly in springtime after the old bark has been completely shed from the stem and the new bark is a fresh deep pink colour. The young foliage is a coppery-red and is popular for indoor use as 'gum tips'.

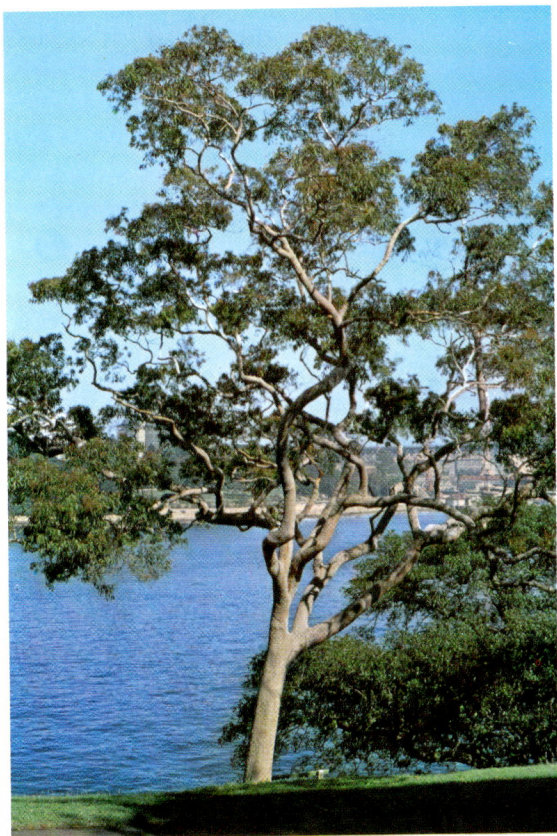

# SPOTTED GUM

*Eucalyptus maculata* (Family Myrtaceae)

HABITAT: The coast of Victoria, N.S.W. and Queensland. Grows in association with other Eucalypts but is more often found in pure stands on stony slopes and valleys in areas with over 20 inch rainfall.

SIZE: Grows to a height of 120 feet with a stem diameter of 4 feet.

DESCRIPTION: Bark is lead-coloured, smooth throughout and spotted; shed in round patches that leave depressions; bark injury often results in extended exudations of Kino. Leaves are lanceolate, 6 inches long, alternate with well-marked veins. Flowers are terminal with sharply pointed bud cap. Fruit is $\frac{1}{2}$ inch long, ovoid and constricted at the neck.

TIMBER: Light brown with wavy grain somewhat like English oak; hard, does not polish well. Used for house construction, parquetry, and very extensively for making tool handles; it is also a good cabinet timber.

GENERAL NOTES: The Spotted Gum generally develops a tall branchless stem and a rather sparse upright crown. Numerous closely-placed small depressions give it a characteristic spotted appearance. It is a poor shade tree but groups of mature trees can be quite spectacular, especially after rain when the stems take on a mottled lustre. The best effects are obtained from groves with a dense background that makes the ornamental stems stand out.

# TUCKEROO

*Cupaniopsis anacardioides* (Family Sapindaceae)

HABITAT: The north coast of N.S.W. and east coast of Queensland, generally on sandy ridges.

SIZE: Grows to 60 feet with a stem diameter of 1 foot but is usually smaller.

DESCRIPTION: Bark is smooth, dark grey in colour. Leaves are pinnate. Leaflets are on $\frac{1}{2}$ inch stalks, 6 to 10, ovate to elliptical, oblong, 3 inches long by $1\frac{1}{2}$ inches broad, rounded at the apex. Flowers are in panicles along the branches. Seed capsules are three-lobed, velvety, 4 inches long and contain oval brown or black seeds enveloped in an orange-red covering. Fruits on some trees are numerous and colourful.

TIMBER: Suitable for heavy cabinet making and tool handles.

GENERAL NOTES: The Tuckeroo is useful for exposed coastal situations as it will grow quite well in sand and can withstand prevailing salt-laden winds. It is handsome throughout the year with dark glossy evergreen foliage and showy fruits during the summer. Because of its hardiness, symmetrical growth and dense branching, it has become popular for street planting and as a shade tree.

# TULIPWOOD

*Harpullia pendula*                              (Family Sapindaceae)

HABITAT: From Bellingen, N.S.W., to Cairns, Q.

SIZE: Attains a height of 80 feet with a stem diameter of 2 feet. The stem is sometimes flanged.

DESCRIPTION: The bark is smooth, brownish-grey, and is shed in irregular long flakes. Young shoots and flowers are downy. Leaves are alternate, elliptical with a blunt point, pinnate with 3 to 6 leaflets, each leaf 3 inches long with a $\frac{1}{4}$ inch stalk; thin veins are prominent underneath. Flowers are on loose, terminal, narrow panicles in the forks of the leaves, greenish-yellow, $\frac{5}{8}$ inch in diameter, not conspicuous. Fruit is a smooth capsule, yellow or reddish, deeply divided into two round lobes, $\frac{1}{2}$ to $\frac{3}{4}$ inch in diameter containing 1 or 2 shiny dark brown or black oval seeds.

TIMBER: Heavy, close-grained, has attractive figure and works easily. The pale yellow sapwood and dark brown heartwood give it strong contrast.

GENERAL NOTES: The Tulipwood is extensively planted as an ornamental evergreen in sub-tropical areas; it develops a globular crown; its dense branching and foliage provides excellent shade. Growth is rapid when it is given good soil and protected from strong winds. It is very ornamental for many weeks at fruiting time but individual trees vary, some bearing only a few fruits with indifferent colouring.

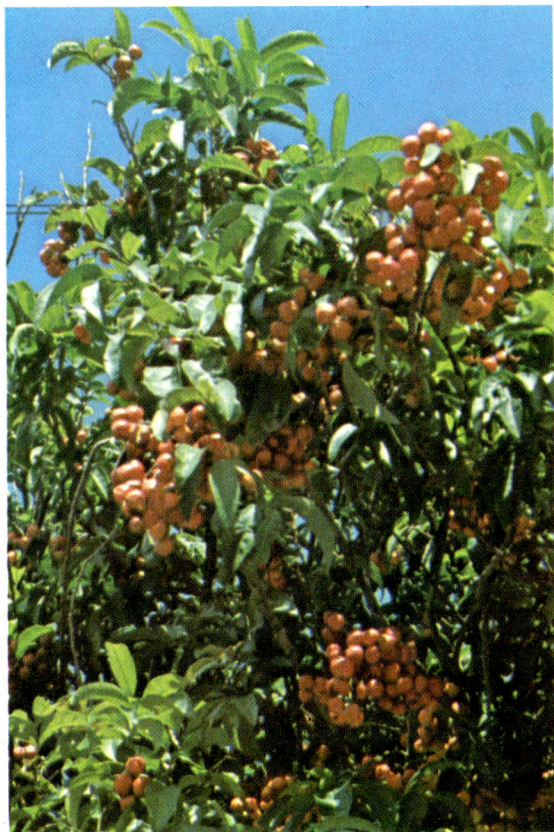

# TURPENTINE

*Syncarpia glomulifera* (Family Myrtaceae)

HABITAT: The Eucalypt forests and the brush forests of the Blue Mountains and coastal districts of N.S.W. and south Queensland, often associated with areas of Wianamatta Shale.

SIZE: Attains a height of 120 feet with a 3 foot stem diameter.

DESCRIPTION: Bark is dark brown, fibrous. Leaves are opposite, ovate to elliptical, 3 inches long; dark green, smooth upper surface, much paler on the underside. Flowers are white and joined at the calyx into dense globular heads. Capsules are fused into a globular head, hard and woody.

TIMBER: Like red ironbark and used almost exclusively for piles, since it is more resistant to the *Toredo* marine borers than other timbers. The bark is invariably left on when used for this purpose because of a resin between the bark and the timber. The timber is also claimed to be resistant to white ants. It is strong, but tends to warp and crack.

GENERAL NOTES: Somewhat resembles the gums but is much denser in foliage and makes a good shade tree when used ornamentally. Under natural conditions it is always found in groups. The foliage is attractive, the contrasting pale undersides of the leaves making a distinctive pattern when seen from underneath or when stirred by a breeze.

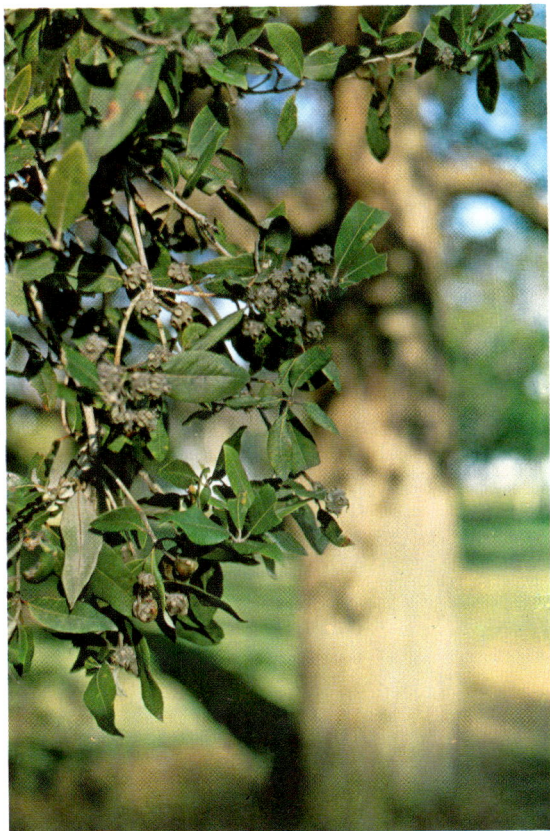

# UMBRELLA TREE

*Schefflera actinophylla* (Family Araliaceae)

HABITAT: The rain forests of northern N.S.W. and Queensland. The genus is limited to a single species which is endemic to Australia. Young leaves bear a strong resemblance to an opened umbrella.

SIZE: Grows to a height of 50 feet with a stem diameter of 18 inches; sometimes buttressed and rarely cylindrical, fluted.

DESCRIPTION: Bark is pale grey, rough-textured. Leaves are radially divided with from 7 to 16 oblong leaflets measuring up to 12 inches by 4 inches, on 3 inch stalks. Flowers are in large terminal heads made of 4 to 8 upright stiff stalks sometimes 2 feet long; the $\frac{1}{2}$ inch red flowers have thick, triangular leathery petals.

TIMBER: Soft, brittle, of no commercial value.

GENERAL NOTES: The Umbrella Tree is used extensively throughout Australia for ornamental planting. It makes an excellent specimen plant. It is evergreen, fast-growing, hardy and quite showy at flowering time which extends from December to February. The large, glossy leaves are handsome and always fresh-looking. Branching is upright, with foliage mostly at the tips; outline is usually that of an inverted cone. The young plants make a most attractive pot plant and it is probably more extensively used for indoor decoration than any other native plant. In its native state it often starts life high up in the forks of other trees. Better known as *Brassaia actinophylla*.

# WEEPING BOTTLEBRUSH

*Callistemon viminalis*                    (Family Myrtaceae)

HABITAT: The east coast of Australia except Victoria, generally bordering freshwater creeks in open forest country.

SIZE: Grows to 60 feet with a stem diameter of 1 foot but is usually much smaller.

DESCRIPTION: The stem is seldom columnar, but twisted and multiple. Bark is dark grey, rough and vertically furrowed. Leaves are linear-lanceolate, 4 inches long, alternate, dark green and smooth; fragrant when crushed. Young leaves are reddish-bronze and covered with downy white hairs. Flowers are in the form of dense terminal spikes with prominent stamens, red in colour and clustered around the central stalk. Growth continues from the central stalk as a leafy shoot, followed by persistent seed capsules with numerous very small papery, light brown seeds.

TIMBER: Of no commercial importance as it is not available in quantity and size is small. It is reddish in colour, close-grained, strong and tough and used for tool handles, boat knees and braces; it is durable underground and has been used for fence posts in damp ground.

GENERAL NOTES: Fast-growing under average conditions and forms into a well-shaped small evergreen tree. During September its drooping branches are covered with brilliant red blooms that are rich in honey and pollen.

# WEEPING MYRTLE

*Syzygium floribundum*                 (Family Myrtaceae)

HABITAT: From N.S.W. to the Northern Territory, usually along and overhanging freshwater streams in scrub land and forest.

SIZE: Grows to 80 feet with a stem diameter of $2\frac{1}{2}$ feet. Stem is sometimes flanged at the base, seldom upright.

DESCRIPTION: Bark is grey and closely furrowed. Leaves are opposite, elliptical, pointed at the apex, 4 inches long, dark green, glossy on both sides. Flowers are in panicles at the ends of the branches or in the axils of the leaves. Individual flowers are small and held on short $\frac{1}{4}$ inch stalks. Calyx is bell-shaped and persists on the globular $\frac{1}{2}$ inch fruit which is fleshy and encloses a cherry-like seed.

TIMBER: Sometimes called Satin Ash, it is tough, close-grained, with wavy grain; suitable for cabinet work.

GENERAL NOTES: The Weeping Myrtle has been grown as a garden tree throughout Australia for many years. Its popularity is due to its willow-like pendulous habit. In damp situations where there is a depth of rich soil, it is fast-growing, developing into a well-shaped evergreen shade tree. After rainy periods the new foliage is a rich burgundy colour. Fruits are attractive but not prominently displayed. Previously known as *Eugenia ventenatii*.

# WEST AUSTRALIAN CHRISTMAS TREE

*Nuytsia floribunda*                    (Family Loranthaceae)

HABITAT: South-western Australia in areas of sandy soil
with a rainfall exceeding 20 inches; usually in groups.

SIZE: Grows to 30 feet with a stem diameter of $1\frac{1}{2}$ feet.

DESCRIPTION: Bark is smooth, reddish brown. Juvenile
leaves are fleshy, one inch long and pointed; mature
leaves are narrow, 4 inches long and $\frac{1}{4}$ inch wide,
without stalks, tapering to the apex and arranged at
about 45 degrees around the branchlets. Flower spikes
are in large clusters, gold-orange, each flower with
6 petals and stamens. The $\frac{3}{4}$ inch papery fruits are
winged and germinate readily while fresh.

GENERAL NOTES: This tree is very beautiful when it is
in flower. From afar it gives the appearance of being
on fire—a good reason for the origin of one of its
common names—the Fire Tree. It has created much
interest because of its parasitic tendencies. As a member
of the Mistletoe family, it relies on other plants to
provide much of its nourishment by tapping their
roots and diverting their nutrients to its own needs.
Nursery seedlings are provided with host plants on
which they depend for survival.

# WHEEL OF FIRE TREE

*Stenocarpus sinuatus* (Family Proteaceae)

HABITAT: Sheltered deep soil coastal scrubs in Queensland and northern N.S.W.

SIZE: Attains a height of 100 feet and a stem diameter of 1 foot.

DESCRIPTION: Bark is dark grey, coarse-textured. Leaves are large, glossy dark green, paler underneath, 7 inches long with 1 inch stalks and deeply lobed on the margins. Flowers are bright red in clusters with several spikes springing from the same branchlet, 10 to 14 flowers form the wheel-like umbel from which the common name is derived. They are followed by clusters of boat-shaped seed pods that contain 2 inch, thin, flattened papery seeds.

TIMBER: Known in the trade as White Beefwood or White Oak. Occasionally used for cabinet making.

GENERAL NOTES: The Wheel of Fire is a very popular ornamental evergreen and flourishes in gardens in all parts of Australia. Some trees are a brilliant red at flowering time (January to March); most trees, however, fail to display the flowers prominently and these give the appearance of a red glow in the dense dark-green foliage. The unopened flowers are regarded as floral curiosities, their structure bears a strong resemblance to the hub and spokes of a car-wheel. It has an upright habit of growth and makes slow growth except under excellent conditions. A related species is *S. salignus*, the Scrub Beefwood.

# WHITE BOTTLEBRUSH

*Callistemon salignus*         (Family Myrtaceae)

HABITAT: South Australia, Victoria, N.S.W. and Queensland in open forest and moist valleys.

SIZE: Will grow to 40 feet but is usually much smaller with a stem that seldom exceeds 10 inches in diameter.

DESCRIPTION: Bark is papery, sometimes rough and closely fissured. Leaves are alternate, leathery, lanceolate, 4 inches long and $\frac{1}{2}$ inch across, smooth on both sides. Flowers are in dense spikes 3 to 4 inches long and $1\frac{1}{2}$ inches in diameter, cream or ivory white, often with a greenish tint. Seed capsule is woody in a cylindrical cluster around the branch where it remains for many months, often until scorched by bush fire when it opens to release the numerous fine brown seeds.

TIMBER: Light pink in colour, close-grained, tough. Lasts well in moist ground. Used in boat building and for fence posts.

GENERAL NOTES: This tree is quite extensively grown as an evergreen ornamental as it is hardy, fast-growing and develops a shapely outline. It makes an attractive floral display in spring; has a few additional blooms during summer. Its main virtue, however, is the production of several flushes of new foliage each year. This is pink or a rich red when seen against the sun; it is often pendant over the whole crown.

# WHITE CEDAR

*Melia azedarach*                    (Family Meliaceae)

HABITAT: The coastal scrubs of north and south Queensland and northern N.S.W.; also New Guinea.

SIZE: Attains a height of 150 feet with a stem diameter of 4 feet; trunk is rounded, seldom buttressed.

DESCRIPTION: Bark is a dark colour and prominently furrowed. Leaves are alternate, pinnate with numerous short-stalked leaflets, each 3 inches long, margins toothed. Flowers are in large panicles springing from the axils of the leaves; they are lilac in colour and measure $\frac{3}{4}$ inch in diameter; blooms in September or October. Fruits are $\frac{1}{2}$ inch oval berries, green then apricot-yellow, with pulp surrounding a hard stone, and are produced in great profusion. They are claimed to be poisonous to animals. Sometimes the seed stones are strung together as beads, giving rise to one of its many common names, Bead Tree.

TIMBER: Highly figured; used as a cabinet wood and in joinery.

GENERAL NOTES: The White Cedar is grown in many Australian gardens. Undoubtedly its wide distribution in suburban gardens can be attributed to the birds that relish its fruits. It is fast-growing, eminently drought-resistant and very adaptable, growing equally well in sandy loam or puggy clay. It is one of the few deciduous trees found in the Australian bush. Sometimes it is defoliated by the Cedar Moth caterpillar.

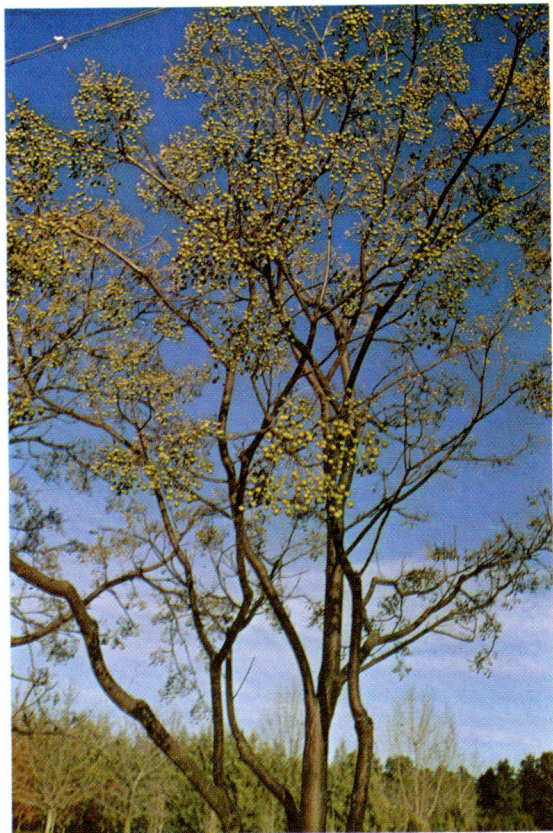

# WHITE GUM

*Eucalyptus mannifera*          (Family Myrtaceae)

HABITAT: The Blue Mountains, N.S.W., down to Victoria, mostly in the highlands on granite or sandstone soils.

SIZE: Grows to 60 feet with a stem diameter of 2 feet.

DESCRIPTION: The new bark is powdery white and smooth to the ground, often a bright pink in early spring; later becomes grey and spotted; flakes off gradually. Mature leaves are dull green on both sides, not glossy, lanceolate, about 4 inches long and narrow with faint venation; they are rich in oil; foliage is usually dense. Flowers are produced between October and December in small heads of 5 to 7 in the axils of the leaves. Capsules are on short stalks, oval in shape with broad outward valves.

TIMBER: Close grained, has a pinkish colour and wavy figure; it has been used for fencing, general purposes and firewood.

GENERAL NOTES: Popular for ornamental use because of its attractive white stem, its hardiness in poor soil, under drought and severe frost conditions. Makes a rounded crown supported by strong sparse branches. Other common names include White Brittle Gum, Cabbage Gum, Red Spotted Gum. Its botanical classification was recently changed from *Eucalyptus maculosa*. It is not related to the true Spotted Gum, *E. maculata*.

# WHITE HONEYSUCKLE

*Banksia integrifolia*          (Family Proteaceae)

HABITAT: The eastern sea coast of Australia and as far inland as the Blue Mountains, N.S.W.

SIZE: Grows to 60 feet with a stem diameter of 1 foot, but is usually a medium sized tree.

DESCRIPTION: Bark is light to dark brown, corded, and rough. Young branches are densely covered with wooly hairs. Leaves are 4 to 8 inches long, on short stalks, leathery, entire, irregularly toothed, sometimes in whorls, with a very close whitish velvety undersurface; veins not prominent. Flowers are upright, bottlebrush-like cones 4 to 8 inches long, 2 inches in diameter, creamy-green in colour. They are honey laden and attract many birds, particularly the Parrakeets. Seed pods are upright, cone-like structures up to 6 inches long, dark brown with prominent individual capsules that gradually open to disperse two papery black seeds.

GENERAL NOTES: The White Honeysuckle is an excellent evergreen tree for ornamental plantings in areas of sandy soil and prevailing winds or in exposed coastal positions. Under such conditions it often develops a gnarled appearance but it can be shapely with dense foliage in less exposed positions. The silvery undersurface of its leaves and often grotesque branching habit, together with its hardiness and rapid growth, commend it as a specimen subject where a special effect is needed.

# WILLOW MYRTLE

*Agonis flexuosa*
(Family Myrtaceae)

HABITAT: Widely distributed along the south-western coastline of Western Australia.

SIZE: Usually attains a height of 30 feet (occasionally 50 feet) and a stem diameter of 2 feet; the stem is seldom vertical.

DESCRIPTION: Slender, crowded and often pendulous branches. Bark is grey, fibrous with vertical fissures. Leaves are alternate, 5 inches long and $\frac{1}{2}$ inch across, smooth, without a stalk, and hang vertically; when crushed they exude a strong peppermint smell. Flowers are stalkless, either in the axils of the leaves or terminal; ivory white and very similar to the Tea-Tree flower (*Leptospermum*). Fruit is a 3-celled capsule that remains on the stem for a long time; it contains numerous fine seeds.

TIMBER: Available only in small sizes; has little commercial value.

GENERAL NOTES: Often referred to as the Willow Peppermint. A very useful tree for coastal planting as it thrives in sandy soil and stands up well to salt laden winds. More often than not it develops a gnarled appearance which gives it an unusual but attractive outline. It has been used as a street tree but as seedlings show considerable variation it is not appropriate for formal effects.

# YELLOW BOX

*Eucalyptus melliodora* (Family Myrtaceae)

HABITAT: Victoria, some isolated small stands in southern Queensland and the tablelands of N.S.W. at 2,000-4,000 feet above sea level in areas of hot, dry summers and cold winters, where the rainfall is as low as 15 inches.

SIZE: Height is up to 100 feet, with a 3 foot stem diameter.

DESCRIPTION: Bark is of dark, hard, flaky strips to half-way up the trunk when it abruptly changes to a smooth apricot-yellow to the branch tips. Leaves are alternate, narrow, 5 inches long, grey-green on both sides; venation not prominent. Buds are club-shaped. Flower panicles are terminal with 3 to 7 flowers. Fruit is ovoid or pear-shaped.

TIMBER: Pale brown, hard, strong, durable and heavy, with interlocked grain. Used mostly for heavy construction but also for sleepers and fencing. Excellent for firewood.

GENERAL NOTES: Yellow Box is regarded as the best honey tree of all the Eucalypts; it flowers profusely throughout the summer. When grown as a solitary specimen it forms a large dense crown from well down the stem making it a well-balanced tree with a graceful framework of strong branches. It is used extensively for ornamental plantings in Victoria and South Australia where many roadsides are lined with it. At times it suffers badly from psyllid attack (Lerp insect).

# YELLOW GUM

*Eucalyptus leucoxylon*             (Family Myrtaceae)
    var. *macrocarpa*

HABITAT: North central Victoria, Port Augusta and the Mt Lofty Ranges in S.A. at altitudes between 500 and 2,000 feet.

SIZE: Grows to 60 feet with a stem diameter of up to $1\frac{1}{2}$ feet; stem is usually short with a loose globular crown.

DESCRIPTION: New bark is grey, smooth; old bark flakes off in large sheets and is rough; persists at the base of the stem where it is hard with deep vertical ridges; Mature leaves are alternate, lanceolate, 6 inches long by 1 inch wide, tapering to a narrow tip; smooth on both sides, midrib prominent; venation at 40 degrees, one-inch stalk. Flowers are on slender stalks in the axils of the leaves in heads of 3; they are deep red, pink or cream in colour, generally drooping; they contain little honey but it is of superior quality. Fruit is pear-shaped; valves are enclosed.

TIMBER: Yellow or pale brown, hard, tough and durable. Used in turnery and in heavy cabinet work, also for pit props.

GENERAL NOTES: A very ornamental gum when in full bloom. Flowering time varies between May and December but in the Monaro district it is in full bloom in April/May, just prior to the early frosts that would spoil the flowers. When raised from seed there is great variation in form and colour. The flowers last well indoors.

129

# INDEX